T0208721

OPERATION RESCUE:
MISSION ACCOMPLISHED

A Bible Study on the Life of Jesus
Based on the Gospel of John

Michelle Harris-Thompson

WESTBOW
PRESS®
A DIVISION OF THOMAS NELSON
& ZONDERVAN

Copyright © 2019 Michelle Harris-Thompson.

All rights reserved. No part of this book may be used or reproduced by any means, graphic, electronic, or mechanical, including photocopying, recording, taping or by any information storage retrieval system without the written permission of the author except in the case of brief quotations embodied in critical articles and reviews.

This book is a work of non-fiction. Unless otherwise noted, the author and the publisher make no explicit guarantees as to the accuracy of the information contained in this book and in some cases, names of people and places have been altered to protect their privacy.

WestBow Press books may be ordered through booksellers or by contacting:

WestBow Press
A Division of Thomas Nelson & Zondervan
1663 Liberty Drive
Bloomington, IN 47403
www.westbowpress.com
1 (866) 928-1240

Because of the dynamic nature of the Internet, any web addresses or links contained in this book may have changed since publication and may no longer be valid. The views expressed in this work are solely those of the author and do not necessarily reflect the views of the publisher, and the publisher hereby disclaims any responsibility for them.

Any people depicted in stock imagery provided by Getty Images are models, and such images are being used for illustrative purposes only.
Certain stock imagery © Getty Images.

Scripture quotations, unless otherwise indicated, are taken from The Holy Bible, New International Version®, NIV® Copyright © 1973, 1978, 1984, 2011 by Biblica, Inc.® Used by permission. All rights reserved worldwide.

Scripture taken from the Amplified® Bible, Copyright © 2015 by The Lockman Foundation. Used by permission.

Scripture taken from The Living Bible, copyright © 1971 by Tyndale House Foundation. Used by permission of Tyndale House Publishers Inc., Carol Stream, Illinois 60188. All rights reserved. The Living Bible, TLB, and the The Living Bible logo are registered trademarks of Tyndale House Publishers.

ISBN: 978-1-9736-4924-3 (sc)
ISBN: 978-1-9736-4923-6 (e)

Print information available on the last page.

WestBow Press rev. date: 12/20/2018

DEDICATION

Increasingly, it is being said that we are living in a post-Christian era. Truth seems to be more about what works for you than related to any fixed standard. Indeed, should one dare to suggest a standard, you do so at the risk of being labelled intolerant and judgmental. Those who look down on us who stand by our faith have the mistaken belief that we checked our brains in at the door; that we are standing on myths and fairy tales.

On the contrary, the Christian way of life is firmly grounded in fact, in a real individual *who actually lived here on earth* and left enough proof for us to make an informed decision. This study is dedicated to those who are not afraid to question, but are also prepared to let go of their preconceived notions and diligently search out the **truth**. In doing so you will find, "You shall know the truth, and the truth shall set you free."

CONTENTS

FOREWORD

Jesus Christ declared in John 17:3, that eternal life, which He came to give (verse 2), is found and results in knowing both the Father and the Son! Essential to this knowing is the careful investigation and disciplined contemplation of the Holy Scriptures, while depending fully upon the Holy Spirit's leading and revelation. Jesus further declared that in carefully perusing these Holy Scriptures which testify of Him, it should inevitably lead us to Him so as to receive the Life He offers! (John 5:39-40). Thus we are constrained to imitate the pattern of the Berean believers who received the Gospel with "...all readiness of mind... [and] searched the Scriptures daily..." to ascertain Truth for themselves. (Acts 17:11) This is one of the main intentions of this book!

Discipline, diligence and detail, the ever-present essentials guiding all serious focus in any area or subject under investigation, are even more of an imperative when considering "...the Apostle and High Priest of our profession, Christ Jesus." (Hebrews 3:1) These features are readily apparent in Michelle Harris-Thompson's approach through these carefully prepared musings, questions and pointers, to help her "students" get to know, understand and receive Jesus, perceive Who He is and receive and affirm what He stands for.

Ultimately His disciples are destined to be found in Jesus' own image and likeness! The direction of this engrossing investigation into Jesus Christ the Son of God HAS, therefore, to lead to the question of HOW for the believer! And herein is the absolute genius of the Lord our God: As we purposefully delve into, examine and contemplate the many, many facets and nuggets of Truth from the Scriptures, and (particularly) the Gospel of John unearthed and shared by Michelle, there must of necessity be a faith response...or many faith responses along the way....to Jesus! That is all He asks!

It's time to begin!

Paul A. Ramsay.

PREFACE

This is a study of Christ's sojourn here on earth in human form. We use the gospel of John as our main source, filling in the gaps with information from the other gospels. It is an attempt to chronicle to some degree the sequence of events as they happened, while getting to know the man, Jesus. As you can well imagine, this is not always possible, but doing so has helped to clear up some apparent contradictions in the Scripture for me. Since this is the aim, there are some things that are obviously not covered by the scope of this study. However, by the time you finish this study, you will have covered the entire book of the Gospel of John.

It is my prayer that these contemplations help to ignite the desire to dig deeper in the Word of God. For this reason, and because each of us may have a preference as to which translation of the Bible we use, I have deliberately avoided printing out the bible passages we will discuss. This means you will need your favourite translation(s) of the Bible as a companion to this study guide. You may also find a notebook, pen and highlighter useful. Unless otherwise stated, quoted Scriptures are taken from the New International Version (NIV) Translation of the Bible.

The study spans 35 chapters and is written so that it may be used for individual quiet time or bible study; or for a group study. If opting for the latter, I would recommend the group chooses one individual as leader who will guide the discussions. In that case, the group could set aside 7 weeks to go through the study, covering 5 chapters per week; each individual doing a chapter a day for 5 days, and then sharing together once per week. I have included some suggestions for discussion points in the group in the appendix at the end of the study. These are just ideas to assist the leader but feel free to choose your own. There are also one or two verses given per week to memorize.

In addition, because I am Jamaican and, as the thoughts flow, oftentimes a Jamaican phrase or word will come to mind that best expresses what I want to say, I have taken the liberty of using them as they come. These are written in italics and are explained immediately in the text.

I hope you find this absorbing subject area as exciting and intriguing as I have. I encourage you to begin each chapter with prayer, asking for the guidance of the Holy Spirit, and the wisdom and understanding of the Lord. As you follow the exercises, meditate on the passages and receive the revelations for yourself **before** continuing into my discussions. The Word of the Lord is true- when you seek Him, you will find Him when you seek Him with all your heart. I invite you to fall in love with Him all over again.

Michelle

ACKNOWLEDGEMENTS

This body of work has been one of faith from start to finish. The Lord thrust me into leading a small home bible study since the late 1990's. When we were nearing the end of this study on the gospel of John, the Lord impressed upon me to prepare this study for publishing. With the encouragement of my very supportive husband, I diligently started doing so in October 2010. Evan, your belief in me and the gift God has given has allowed my faith to grow. The first draft was completed in November 2011. A dear friend, mentor and brother in Christ, Mr. Paul Ramsay, offered to edit and faithfully went through in detail, offering corrections, insight and advice. This took a year to complete. I can never express sufficiently how grateful I am for his diligence and willingness to put so much of his time into this work. Paul, I pray the Lord will bless you abundantly for your sacrifice. You made me believe this could really happen!

I would also like to thank those who have been faithful to the call of God on their lives in teaching me how to dig deeper in the Word and to test what I learn, in particular Pastor Rawle Tyson, Pastor Al Miller and my teachers at Whole Life Ministries. My friend and fellow worker in Christ, Peter Malcolm, who saw the gift in me and left me to lead the home bible study: Look what the Lord has done! To all who shared these years of bible study with me, thank *oonu* for the lessons learnt, and for allowing iron to sharpen iron.

Above all, thanks and praise to Almighty God, and my Lord and precious Saviour, Jesus Christ: how true – "We have this treasure in jars of clay to show that this all-surpassing power is from God and not from us." It is the Lord's doing and it is marvellous in our eyes!

INTRODUCTION

It has been said that one of the distinguishing features between Christianity and other religions is that the latter usually involve man reaching out for god while with Christianity, God reaches out to man. From the creation of Adam and Eve, God has sought relationship with mankind. With the "fall" and the expulsion of man from God's presence, God set about His plan to restore our connection with Him. Genesis 1: 26 declared:

"Then God said, 'Let **us** make man in **our** image, in **our** likeness...'" and verse 27 states that God did make mankind (male and female) in His image...and it was very good. Then came sin and the fall and, by Genesis 5, in verse 1 we read that man **was** made in the likeness of God, but then verse 3 points out that when Adam was 130 years, he had a son in **his** own likeness, in **his** own image'. In other words, all mankind was subsequently born in sin, in the likeness of Adam after he had disobeyed God; hence our need to be 'born again' (John 3:3).

Yet even as God declared the respective curses on Adam, Eve, and the serpent, we see in the midst of it, the promise of redemption as Genesis 3:15 declared to the serpent '[the seed of the woman] will crush your head, and you will strike his heel' – a prophecy fulfilled in Jesus' victory over Satan. So from the beginning the promise of the Deliverer is certain.

From Adam to Noah, man multiplied, as did his corruption, so God wiped the slate clean, starting afresh with the only group of believers: Noah and his family. Again, as mankind multiplied and populated the earth, it was God who again introduced Himself to Abram (a descendant of Noah's son

Shem), setting in motion His plan that would see a people distinct from those around them, drawing others unto God. A people who would be taught the ways of God, who would have relationship with God, and who would demonstrate His power and distinctiveness by being different… set apart. From Abram (later called Abraham) to Isaac, and Isaac to Jacob (later Israel), God revealed Himself, and declared the promise of a nation whose God is the Lord. God intervened in history to draw mankind to Himself.

To Jacob's offspring, the nation of Israel, God again reached out, powerfully delivering them from slavery in Egypt; writing with His own hand His laws and requirements, and providing a land to settle in… intervening in history to draw mankind unto Himself.

DID YOU KNOW?
Abraham purchased his own piece of land in Canaan, the Promised Land… to bury his wife Sarah.
Genesis 23.

Repeatedly man, born into sin, rebelled against God, seeking to rule his own destiny. After conquering and settling in the Promised Land, the Israelites would repeatedly rebel against God. The constant refrain in the book of Judges was "In those days Israel had no king; everyone did as he saw fit". Again and again, God would raise up judges to lead the people, freeing them from bondage and persecution- intervening in history to draw mankind unto Himself. Then God called Samuel to be His voice and to guide Israel, but the people refused to be satisfied. They wanted to be like the other nations and demanded a king- not recognizing that God Himself was their King, rebelling against the very thing that set them apart.

So they were given Saul, whom God later rejected; then David- "a man after God's own heart" – imperfections and all, but who to this day remains Israel's most beloved and revered king. Under David, the kingdom expanded and under Solomon, his son, it prospered and gained wealth and acclaim. But the seeds of insurrection were evident in the many foreign wives and their idolatrous religions. With Solomon's death, the kingdom became divided into the Southern kingdom, which comprised mostly the tribes of Judah and Benjamin ruled by David's descendants and centred around Jerusalem; and the Northern kingdom which was comprised of the remainder of the 12 tribes- also called Israel. Both kingdoms were ruled by a series of kings who led the people of God into idolatry and practices detestable to God. Only in Judah (the Southern kingdom) were there occasions where a godly king would rise up and lead the people to repentance and return to God. Repeatedly, God called prophets to be His voice, intervening in history to draw Mankind unto Himself. Rarely did His people listen; more often they ignored or harmed the messengers.

Eventually, the Northern Kingdom was taken into captivity by Assyria in 722 BC. Some years later, the Southern Kingdom was conquered by Babylon (in ~ 586 BC). Even in exile, God continued to send prophets like Jeremiah and Ezekiel to speak His words of promise and encouragement to His covenant people - declaring the period of captivity to be 70 years and pointing out that even their captors were but His instruments. Babylon was subsequently conquered by the Medes and Persians and Cyrus, King of Persia repatriated the Jews- God intervening in history. Ezra and Nehemiah returned to lead and help in the rebuilding of Jerusalem.

So the Old Testament ends with the Jews under Persian rule. The subsequent years not elaborated on were in fact prophesied about in Daniel (Chapters 7, 8 and 9). Approximately 400 years separate the Old Testament from the New.

After the Persians, the Greek Empire ruled and, while the Persians had tried to resettle the exiles in their respective countries and allowed them to worship their own gods, this was not the case with Alexander the Great. He instituted a process called Hellenization in which the captives were to essentially follow Greek culture and be united by the Greek language. His successors (the primary ones being the Ptolemies and the Seleucids) followed the same practice. While the Ptolemies had been tolerant of Jewish practices, the Seleucids were determined to eradicate them. In particular Antiochus IV Epiphanes (title meaning 'God made manifest') carried out radical Hellenization, among other things- erecting a statue of Zeus and sacrificing a pig (such sacrilege) in the Jerusalem temple.[1] He tried to force the Jews to abandon their religious practices and offer sacrifices to pagan gods in his determination to destroy all worship of the one true God.[2]

This resulted in a rebellion led by Matthathias and his five sons, most prominently Judas (Maccabeus) called the Maccabean revolt, a 24 year war which led to the independence of Judah until the Romans took control.[1] So by the time Jesus arrives on the scene, the Jews are under Roman rule. Distressing, yes?...but God's perfect timing! God had established the Hebrew people as the chosen caretakers of His law, to demonstrate Himself to the world and to point nations to Him. With Greek domination and Hellenization, there was a common language- Greek, and Roman rule brought with it a very ordered political and social structure, and an extensive road network.

God at just the right time sent Jesus- when His Word had been given to the Jews, now with a universal language to communicate that Word, and the means to spread it to the nations through the ordered social structure and road network. God intervenes in history to draw mankind unto Himself.

CHAPTER 1
THE WORD

READ JOHN 1: 1 – 3
Read it again, slowly. Think about what it is saying. Write down your
thoughts. _____

_____

_____

The Greek word translated as 'word' here is LOGOS. Vine's Complete
Expository Dictionary of Old and New Testament Words (Vine's)
elaborates that this denotes:

1. the expression of thought…as embodying a conception or idea by
    God or by Christ,
2. the revealed will of God, and
3. the title of the Son of God.

READ GENESIS 1: 1 – 3a
Consider the two passages together. Both start off "In the beginning"…
before all creation, before time began. Here in Genesis, the Hebrew
word 'Elohim' is translated 'God'. Elohim is plural (singular El) but the
verb 'created' is singular. Vine's and some other commentaries state that
this term Elohim is a plural of majesty[3], expressing intensification rather
than number[4] (akin to the royal "We"). Nevertheless, Genesis 1: 26 – 27
reasserts the notion of more than one, for God says, " Let **_us_** make man

in *our* image, in *our* likeness…". Now then, look again at the first three verses of Genesis 1 and let us compare them with John 1: 1. In Genesis we are told that Elohim created the heavens and the earth. John 1: 1 tells us that the Word was *with* God (distinct from God), yet *was* God. Most of us have always interpreted the Genesis passage as speaking only of God "the Father", the Almighty. Genesis mentions the Spirit of God hovering or moving over the waters. The only clear evidence of the Word (that John 1: 1 says was there in the beginning) is, 'and God **said**, "Let there be…"'. What is my point? Simply that the evidence of the Triune God - a term not found in Scripture and a concept very hard for our limited minds to grasp - is there from the beginning. I don't believe it is a coincidence that the term used for the Creator in John 1 is the WORD.

Just as the Holy Spirit is as much God as He is a part of the 'God-Head', and it is the Spirit of God given to us that enables us to know and understand the mind of God [1 Corinth. 2: 11], so is the Word as much God as He is a part of the God-Head. God opened His mouth, spoke, and the Word came forth and did the creating. I believe that is why "the Word of God is living and active. Sharper than any two-edged sword, it penetrates even to dividing soul and spirit, joints and marrow; it judges the thoughts and attitudes of the heart. Nothing in all creation is hidden from God's sight." [Hebrews 4: 12 – 13a].

Look back at JOHN 1: 1 – 3.

John unequivocally states that the Word was there in the beginning, pre-existing time and all creation and, from the outset, he declares that not only was the Word with God, but He **was** also God!

What else do you notice verse 3 saying?

_____

_____

That's right- it was through the Word that all, **everything!!** was made. *Notn neva mek widout im* (Nothing was made without Him) i.e. once it exists, He made it!

READ COLOSSIANS 1: 13 – 17 and HEBREWS 1: 1 – 3

Who are these passages referring to? _____

Who is credited with creation? _____

From these passages, how would you describe the Son of God?

_____

_____

_____

Do you sense His power and authority? Can you feel the awe? Are you amazed at His Glory? Just think, not only did He make everything...His very word is what is **sustaining** everything (and you are included in that "everything")! [Col. 1: 17, Heb. 1: 3]. Stop and think about that!!

READ REVELATION 19: 11 – 16

Who is this passage referring to? _____

What do you learn from verse 13? _____

READ JOHN 1: 4 – 18

Who is the John mentioned here in verse 6? _____

What do we learn from verses 10 & 11?_____

Who do you think verse 11 is referring to i.e. who were 'His own'?

_____

_____

We are assured by the writer of John's gospel that John the Baptist was sent from God Himself to testify/ bear witness/ confirm the truth of the identity of the 'Word '. God left nothing to chance. *Yu kyaan se yu neva ier or dat nobadi neva tel yu!* (You cannot say you were not told). Yet creation never recognized its Creator. Indeed, even the very people in whom God had deposited His laws and to whom He had promised a Messiah/ Saviour- yes, even the Jewish people themselves rejected the 'Word'.

From the passages:

Who is the Word? _____

What other words have been used here to describe Him? _____

What is available to us because of Him? _____

What does that mean to you? _____
_____

In our study thus far, then, we have seen that the 'Son of God' is the Word- made flesh, is the image of the invisible God and is the **exact** representation of His very being. He was present in the beginning and is not only the Creator of all things but the sustainer of all things. He is the means by which we are reconciled to God, giving us the right to become children of God. He is God's only begotten (One and Only) Son, the King of kings and Lord of lords. John the Baptist testified of Him, confirming that He existed before him (John), though He came after John. *He is Jesus Christ, the One and Only, full of grace and truth!*

Let us close this session by meditating again on verse 12: *(Memory verse)*

> *"Yet to all who received Him, to those who believed in His Name, He gave the right to become children of God."* [*John 1: 12*]

PRAYER: -
Father, what an awesome gift and privilege- to no longer be separated from You but rather to be Your family, *Yu pikni* (Your children), with all the rights (and responsibilities) that come with that. Thank You for thinking about us, even while we were far from You.

CHAPTER 2
HIS ANCESTRY

Now friends, we are about to take a walk through the genealogy of Jesus Christ- something many of us often jump over to get to the " interesting stuff"... but bear with me. I promise we will discover a rich treasure of gems in our searching and studying.

Before we start, however, there are some things to note. We tend to consider family trees and genealogies as set structures that clearly flow from one generation to the next. However, in the Bible, these were more flexible. For example, John Brown may be said to be the father of Tom but in reality the former may be the great- great- great- grandfather of Tom but because of the aim of the writer, the intervening generations are omitted. It is not incorrect, for in the writer's eyes, John Brown is the ancestor of Tom and, therefore, his father. This explains why King David was often referred to as "the father of ..." especially in the books of Kings and Chronicles. In 2 Kings 18: 1 – 3 we read where Hezekiah became king of Judah and did right in the eyes of the Lord, just as his *father* David had done. Now David had lived many generations before King Hezekiah and, in fact, Ahaz was actually Hezekiah's father. However the writer was pointing out that Hezekiah was upright before the Lord, like his ancestor David (and unlike his immediate predecessor Ahaz).

So too in Matthew, as we are about to read, the writer selected the relevant ancestors so as to get groups of fourteen generations- fourteen being a multiple of seven. The number seven (and its multiples) held significance for Jews, being the number of completeness, and fourteen was also the numerical value of David's name (i.e. the Hebrew letters in the name David add up to that number).[5]

READ MATTHEW 1: 1 – 16 and compare and contrast with LUKE 3: 23 – 38. Write down the things that stand out to you in each passage first, then the differences and similarities between the two.

_____
_____
_____
_____
_____
_____
_____
_____
_____
_____
_____
_____
_____
_____

Points of note:-

Matthew

1. Matthew focuses on the connection in Jesus' lineage to David and Abraham.
2. Four women (along with Mary) are high-lighted in Matthew's genealogy- Tamar, Rahab, Ruth and Uriah's wife (Bathsheba). This is unusual in a patriarchal society.
3. As said before, Matthew stresses fourteen generations from Abraham to David, from David to the Babylonian exile and from the exile to Jesus.
4. Matthew carries Jesus' lineage through the kings of Judah (David → Solomon → …. Josiah – (see the books of Kings and Chronicles).

Luke

1. Luke traces Jesus' lineage all the way back to Adam and ends with Him being the son of God.
2. Though the four women mentioned in Matthew are not named in Luke, each had a son included in Luke's record and so remain ancestors of Jesus.
3. The names from Abraham to David are identical in both gospels. After David, the names are different.

Odd, isn't it?! How can that be? Our first response might be "Clearly, there is an error!"…but no- let us put things into context. Matthew was a Jew and geared his gospel/ testimony to the Jews. Abraham was considered the father of the Jewish nation. This is why Matthew traces Jesus' line back to Abraham. In addition, Messiah was not only to be the seed of Abraham but must be born of David's line. He would be the king to come and sit on David's throne – hence Matthew's tracing of the royal line through the kings of Judah.

Luke, on the other hand, was a Gentile and therefore, followed Jesus' parentage back to Adam, the ancestor of the whole human race. Matthew wanted to prove to the Jews that Jesus was indeed the long-awaited Messiah. Luke wanted to demonstrate that He qualified to save the whole world. Fine … but why such a big difference between the two records after David?

Some believe that each writer just selected the names from the ancestral pool, choosing the ones that most suited his goal. Another view is that one line followed the biological line of Joseph while the other, that of the legal father. Let me explain: -

Deuteronomy 25: 5 – 6 issues a command concerning the responsibility of a man to his brother's widow, if his brother died without a son to carry on his name and inherit his estate. He must marry her and their first son would **legally** belong to his brother (though **biologically** be his). This is called the Levirate law. The custom however, preceded the law, because we find it played out as early as Genesis 38 where Judah's daughter-in-law experiences the death of two husbands (Judah's sons) without having a child. Judah promises to her his third son when he is old enough, but reneges on his promise. In light of that custom, we see why her actions were considered "righteous" [verse 26] and not scandalous (as we would interpret it in our society). She was seeing to the preservation of her husband's name and family line, and her own security.

BRAATA (a little something extra): This concept of a brother (kinsman) redeeming his brother's (relative's) name and property is also seen in Ruth 3 and 4, though here the relative was more distant than a brother.

Thus, in the genealogy of Jesus, it is **suggested** that Heli (though listed as Joseph's father in Luke) died childless and his half-brother Jacob married his widow, who then conceived and gave birth to Joseph (Mary's husband). Therefore, Jacob would be Joseph's **biological** father (and named as such in Matthew) but Heli would be his **legal** father (listed as such by Luke). Heli's line traces to Nathan (son of David and Bathsheba), Jacob's line goes back to Solomon (another son of David and Bathsheba)[6].

Others (and I am more inclined to agree with these) believe Luke followed the lineage of Mary since Joseph was not really Jesus' father- hence Luke stressing in verse 23 "He was the son, *so it was thought*, of Joseph". They assert that Jesus, through Mary, was a biological descendant of Nathan, son of David. Through Joseph, He was the legal heir of the kingly birthright from the line of Solomon, son of David.[7] This seems to have further confirmation from a source outside the bible, the Jerusalem Talmud (Haggigah, book 77, 4) where Mary is said to be the daughter of Heli, which would make Joseph the son-in-law of Heli. Thus, Joseph could rightfully be called the son of Heli by Jewish standards.[8] In my opinion, Luke's intimate knowledge of the circumstances concerning Mary's visitation by the angel and other events in Mary's life suggests that he got some of his information directly from Mary (or her family). Matthew however, being Jewish, would trace the ancestral tree through Jesus' legal father, Joseph. What do you think?

Regardless of which record you follow, both genealogies establish that:-

• Jesus, at least regarding His ancestry, qualifies to be Messiah as He was a descendant of Abraham and born of David's line. In fact, at various times in the Scriptures, we see individuals addressing Him as the Son of David and none of His enemies seemed to ever deny this, bearing in mind that His records would have been easily accessible at the temple during His lifetime.

• Tamar, Rahab, Ruth and Bathsheba are ancestors of Jesus. In Luke, Nathan (son of David and Bathsheba- c.f. 1 Chron. 3: 5) is included instead of Solomon (son of David and Bathsheba). I have to ask myself why would God ensure that the records point them out? After all, Sarah wasn't mentioned; neither Rachel nor Leah. Why highlight these women? Tamar- a faithful widow seeking her rights in preserving her husband's name, having been rejected by her father-in-law and put to shame in the eyes of her family and neighbours; Rahab- a prostitute who chose to stand with God's people and later became the wife of Salmon and mother of Boaz; Ruth- a Moabitess- scorned by Jews but who still leaves her country, her home and religion to follow Naomi and her God; and Bathsheba- a wife seduced into adultery through the invitation (command?) of King David, who subsequently becomes pregnant causing David to orchestrate the death of her husband … yet, of all the many, *many* wives of David, she is chosen by God to bear the sons who will be Messiah's ancestors. It almost seems like God is saying, "It doesn't matter your past. I choose the foolish things, the weak things. What others reject, ridicule, scorn, judge and laugh at- I love, accept and transform for their good and to bring Me glory!" Hallelujah!

BRAATA: -
Be encouraged to study the lives of these aforementioned women. What can we learn from them?

- Finally, I believe Matthew stresses the sets of fourteen generations, signifying completeness, because Jesus' coming represented a New Beginning!

Gentle people, I hope you have not gotten lost among the waves of history and culture. Did you ever expect that such a long list of "hard to pronounce" names could hold so much treasure? I trust that you are seeing the clear evidence of God's hand and purpose. Isn't it wonderful to dig deeper?!

PRAYER: -
Lord, in Your very Word is the clear evidence of Your control and Your faithfulness. Thank You that You can take my past and all of who I am and transform me into a testimony to Your love, mercy and grace. I look at all the "skeletons" in Jesus' closet and realize You can also transform my family. Thank You. Please cause us, like Jesus, to bring glory to Your Name.

CHAPTER 3
THE FORERUNNER

There are a number of passages in the Old Testament that foretell things concerning the coming of Messiah. Some speak of a "Day of the Lord" that is understood to be the final judgment on the peoples of this world. Many of these passages speak to a partial fulfillment in the more immediate sense while declaring what is to be in the "end times". One such passage is this:

READ MALACHI 4: 1 – 6
What thoughts come to mind concerning this passage?

_____

_____

The Jewish scholars of Jesus' day believed that, based on this passage, Elijah must come before Messiah appears. In his day, Elijah had gone about preaching repentance and Elisha who declared judgment and deliverance succeeded his ministry. Both were prophets to the Northern Kingdom of Israel during the times of the kings. The Jews therefore, were expecting Elijah to appear and his coming would be an indicator of Messiah's appearing.

READ LUKE 1: 5 – 25
Starting at verse 5, make notes of the things that stand out to you in this passage. _____

_____

_____

_____

Which tribe of Israel did Zechariah and his wife belong to? _____
Given their situation described in verse 7, and their relationship with God
outlined in verse 6, what do you think would have been their feelings and
actions concerning their childless state?

_____

_____

_____

Look at verses 8 – 10. Picture the setting.
Describe the sights, sounds and scents.

_____

_____

_____

_____

How do you think Zechariah felt?

_____

_____

Verse 12 describes how he felt when the angel appeared- what thoughts
do you think went through his mind?

_____

_____

What does the angel prophesy concerning John?

_____

_____

Describe what you believe Zechariah was feeling on hearing these words
of the angel? _____

_____

What do you think the people outside were thinking while waiting for
Zechariah to reappear? _____

_____

Think about and describe the reunion of Elizabeth and her husband on
his return home. Picture him relaying to her the event in the temple. Put
yourself in her shoes – how would you feel?

_____

_____

Zechariah and Elizabeth must have longed for children as every Jewish, indeed, most couples in general do. As the years passed, no doubt their hopes must have waned. The Bible does not say how old they were, only that they were well along in years. It is noteworthy to me that it did not say she was past the age of child-bearing (as had been said of Sarah in Genesis), but certainly in Zechariah's mind, the situation now seemed impossible [verse 18] and, despite the awe of an actual visitation of an angel, he just couldn't see it happening (notice what the angel said in verse 20). Yet, from the angel's opening words, Zechariah had been praying for just that. We can't say if it was his prayer at that moment or if it had been his prayer over the years, but note it, when the answer came, it did "at the proper time" [verse 20]!

I can almost feel the longing of this couple- wanting to believe but afraid to get their hopes up after so long; the unbridled joy when this gift seems certain and the awe of this great God, Yahweh, taking time to stop and *preke pan dem* (notice/ remember them), granting them the longing of their hearts. Can't you just savor the overflowing thankfulness in their hearts? Consider Elizabeth's words in verse 25 – acknowledging the Lord's doing. Isn't it marvellous?!

Note especially verse 17 and recall what we just read in Malachi chapter 4. When we read the bible, we may not be aware that approximately 400 years separate the Old and New Testaments. There was no "word from the Lord", no prophet rising up to declare "Thus saith the Lord…". The generation into which John and Jesus were born could only listen to, as children, and later read stories about the prophets of old. Indeed some may even have scoffed at those accounts, considering them mere fairy tales. No wonder the need for a John- one who would turn "the disobedient to the wisdom of the righteous- to make ready a people prepared for the Lord" [Luke 1: 17]. All Israel needed to have their hearts softened (the field ploughed) to receive what the Lord was about to say and do among them. Isn't the Lord gracious indeed?!!

BRINGING IT HOME: -

Pause here for a moment. Is there anything the Lord may be saying to you as you consider Zechariah and Elizabeth's story?

READ JOHN 1: 19 – 28
What are your comments?

_____

_____

_____

In 2 Kings 2, Elijah the prophet is taken up to heaven in a whirlwind while Elisha looks on. Elijah therefore, did not experience death. The Jews therefore, believed that this same Elijah would return to announce Messiah's coming and the final judgment. John freely denies being both the Messiah and the prophet Elijah. He does, however, echo the words of Isaiah 40: 3 which indicate he is preparing the way for the Lord. Take note, he did say to his hearers that the Christ was right then "among" them i.e. here [vs. 26 & 27].

READ MARK 9: 2 – 13
What do you think this record served to establish?_____
What would Peter, James and John have concluded by the end of Verse 8?

_____

What do verses 9 & 10 tell you? _____
Look again at vs. 11 – 12. Who do you think Jesus was referring to?

_____

Compare with Matthew's testimony:

READ MATTHEW 17: 1 – 13
What added information is given here? _____

The coming of Jesus Christ ushers in a new era and begins the fulfillment of many of the Old Testament (O.T.) prophecies. The ultimate fulfillment will be His second coming in judgment and the establishing of a new heaven and a new earth, but many events are 'compacted' in the prophecies. Malachi prophesies that God will know who is His when He comes in judgment and takes up His "treasured possession". The evildoers will be cast into the lake of fire. However, it seems the first and second comings, respectively, of Christ are compacted and Malachi prophesies that Elijah will come first.

> **BRAATA: -**
> **Look at Revelation 11. Many believe Elijah is one of the two witnesses.**

The Pharisees knew the law (O.T.) and so they knew to expect Elijah before the Messiah, hence their questions to John. John does not appear to consider himself to be Elijah but clearly Christ does. The three disciples, having heard the witness of God from the cloud (confirming their belief that Jesus was the Christ, and commanding them to now focus on and **heed** this Living Word, who supercedes the Law and Prophets – represented by Moses and Elijah), are left confused because they were taught that Elijah must come first. Jesus affirms that he **had** come (in the person of John the Baptist- as the angel had foretold Zechariah) but he was not recognized and so was mistreated, imprisoned and beheaded. In the same way, Jesus the Christ would also not be recognized and so would suffer and be rejected (as was also foretold). Did you notice that Jesus clearly told them he would die and be resurrected but it seems denial is a strong force- apparently they just could not wrap their brains around that … they weren't ready to hear it.

What about you, my friend? Has God been telling you something you don't really want to hear right now? Could He be answering a prayer you have long prayed, but not in the way or the time you expected? Does the way you see yourself line up with the way God perceives you?

PRAYER: -
Father, forgive me for not listening to You, especially when You are saying what I don't want to hear! Grant me a submissive spirit. I know You desire the best for me and will grant all at the proper time. Help me to be patient and not lose hope. Help my unbelief. Thanks for Your mercy and Your grace.

CHAPTER 4

THE PROMISE

❧ ✻ ❧

READ LUKE 1: 26 – 45

In the sixth month of what [vs.26]? _____

What do you think of Mary's response and how does it compare with Zechariah's response? _____

_____

Why do you think Gabriel mentioned Elizabeth?

_____

What occurs at the meeting between Mary and Elizabeth?

_____

_____

Now look at Mary's song of thanksgiving: -

READ LUKE 1: 46 – 56

I used to wonder at God's treatment of Zechariah compared to that of Mary. Zechariah questioned and was struck dumb. Mary questioned but was given an explanation and even a testimony as to the fulfilling of another seemingly impossible occurrence- her old 'barren' relative was now six months pregnant. Why the disparity in treatment? Was it because Zechariah was an old priest of God and should know better but Mary was a young innocent child? Though it is possible that God could have been treating each of them based on their knowledge of Him ("From everyone who has been given much, much will be demanded"- Luke 12:

48), it seems here that it is more a question of God knowing the heart. Both questioned – but Zechariah really did not believe [Luke 1: 20]. Mary, however, did [Luke 1:45]. It says to me there is nothing wrong with questioning, but how blessed is the heart that trusts God to do what He said He would. Notice Mary's quick response as the angel clears up her confusion [vs. 38] - "I am the Lord's servant". The words out of Elizabeth's mouth must have encouraged and strengthened her because Mary had only uttered a greeting, had not sought any confirmation, had not even shared her experience of the visitation, yet Elizabeth could ask "Why am I so favoured that the mother of my Lord should come to me?"

Isn't God gracious- to provide this for a young girl who surely must be overwhelmed by the task set before her? We can only guess her thoughts- "How do I explain this to Joseph? What will people say? Help me, Lord!". Elizabeth's words must have been a balm flooding her mind with relief. No wonder her heart would overflow with a song of praise and thanksgiving. "Yahweh was faithful. This was His doing- to accomplish what He had long promised and Israel had long looked for …and through a lowly *sumadi* (somebody) like me."

Take note of the fact that Mary went to visit Elizabeth when the latter was six months pregnant and stayed with her three months. I would like to believe she stayed until Elizabeth gave birth- getting a first-hand experience of what she too would very soon go through (and that with only Joseph to help)- good preparation.

READ MATTHEW 1: 18 – 25
What thoughts do you have as you compare Joseph's experience with Mary's?_____

_____

These verses depict the very real dilemma Joseph was faced with. In Jewish custom, the betrothal was as binding as a marriage- notice Joseph was already considered her husband [vs. 19] – quite unlike our present Western culture. Mary could lawfully face death by stoning for allegedly committing adultery [Deut. 22: 23 – 27]. We get a glimpse of Joseph's heart- not puffed up with pride and demanding vengeance but rather seeking to protect Mary, though clearly not believing her story... until confirmed by the angel of the Lord. Note his immediate response- he did what the Lord commanded. God found in this couple hearts ready to serve, even at a cost to themselves- can't you just hear the wagging tongues of the gossipmongers?

Note again the differences in the details recounted in the two gospels. Matthew needed to ensure the whole thing was right in Jewish eyes- he stressed the vision to Joseph, the head of the household (and a son of David [vs. 20]). Luke on the other hand, focusing on Jesus' link to the whole human race, gave his attention to Mary, since it was not Joseph's son but God's.

Let's end today by looking at the birth of John the Baptist.

READ LUKE 1: 57 – 80
Again, record your insights.

_____

_____

_____

_____

People are people no matter where or what era. A mother declares that her newborn baby is to be called John but the crowd *no link it rait* (they disagree) and so want Zechariah to set it straight. I am aware that in this patriarchal society, the naming of a child, especially a first-born son is the prerogative of the father – all the more likely that Elizabeth's public declaration would have already been sanctioned and ratified by her husband. I have to smile at verse 63 as I picture the "astonishment" of the people when he sides with his wife! (Don't we just love to dictate to others what they should do!)?

Gabriel had told Zechariah that he would not be able to speak until the day his message was fulfilled. Yet, John was eight days old before Zechariah's tongue was loosed. It happened only after he publicly acknowledged (to a crowd of witnesses) that this was the Lord's doing, by naming his son 'John' in obedience to the angel's command. Do you realize that this would be the first time in nine months that Zechariah was finally able to voice his experience of his visitation by an angel and confirm with his own mouth what God had declared to him through the angel Gabriel? Now do you see why it had the whole hill country of Judea talking? After almost 400 years of silence, God had spoken.

Zechariah had had nine months to ponder the words of the angel. As a priest of God, he knew the prophecies concerning Messiah. From his song of praise we see that he recognized Messiah would soon be here (no doubt Mary would have shared with him and Elizabeth what the angel had told her). Redemption- freedom from their oppressors and return to Israel's sovereignty, the long held desire of every Jew- was clearly in his thoughts as we look at verses 69 – 75. He realized that John was indeed the long awaited 'Elijah' who would prepare the way. Peace would soon be theirs. As they basked in their joy, I doubt that he and Elizabeth had any inkling of what John was in for.

PRAYER:
Father, I am so grateful that You still speak. Help me to come aside from the noise of the daily urgencies and must-dos so I can hear Your still small voice. Grant me strength and courage too, Lord, to not only hear but to obey.

CHAPTER 5
IMMANUEL, GOD WITH US

Gentle people, we now turn to the record of Jesus' birth- a story often told in song, drama, movies as well as from pulpits and storybooks. Along the way, some embellishments and misconceptions have resulted. So now I ask you to put aside, forget if possible, what you may have heard, seen or read and look with fresh eyes and an open mind as we return to the Source of the greatest story ever told.

READ LUKE 2: 1 – 20
Have you ever wondered why Joseph was accompanied by Mary? After all, she was pregnant and very near delivery- why put her through such an arduous journey (believed to be at least a three day trip), away from family who could have been there to help with her delivery? The simple answer is Mary too needed to register [vs.5] – for she too was of David's line.

True, she placed the baby in a manger- a feeding trough for the animals but the Scripture did not say that cattle and sheep (and any number of other farm animals) were there- that is an assumption. All the lovely Christmas card scenes of shepherds kneeling in the snow gazing at the star are also assuming the season. The shepherds were "living out in the fields"- this makes it less likely that there was snow but the fact is we do not know what time of year it was.

Regardless, God pulled out all the stops. Like any proud father, He joyfully spread the news of His Son's birth. An angel of the Lord, with the Glory of God shining all around plus a great company of heavenly host lifting praise to God beats fireworks in my book. The angel declared "good news of great joy...*for all people*"- rich and poor, male and female, Jew and Gentile- good news indeed! Messiah, Christ has come! Notice the proof: you will find the baby in a manger...HUH? Messiah? ... In a manger? ... not a palace?...But what a good thing- otherwise it is unlikely these lowly shepherds would have been given the opportunity to see Him. I believe this is significant because Messiah is available to everyone. All heaven was rejoicing in amazement at what God had done ... become man-Immanuel; but do not bypass the last few words of the angels' "song"- "On earth peace to men *on whom His favour rests*.

What do you think that meant? _____
_____
_____
_____

Lasting, inner peace comes to the one who has made peace with God, received by faith in Christ. It is not promised to all. After the shepherds saw Him, they testified- spreading the word. The response to meeting the Saviour should be telling others about Him. No doubt, they shared with Mary and Joseph how it was that they came to look for Jesus ... and this young mother "treasured up and pondered them in her heart". I'm sure as the years wore on and as the child Jesus grew she would reflect on all these things.

READ LUKE 2: 21 – 38
What have you learnt? _____
_____
_____
_____

- Like Zechariah and Elizabeth, Joseph and Mary acted on the angel's instructions, demonstrating their faith in God- in this instance, the child is given the name "Jesus"- a Name that today still has power when uttered in faith.

- His parents (and subsequently He Himself) followed all the requirements of the law. Hence Jesus was circumcised on the eighth day and consecrated to the Lord as the first-born male.

- The sacrifice that the law required [vs. 24] is spelled out in Leviticus 12. Thirty-three days after Jesus was circumcised, Joseph and Mary took Jesus to the temple in Jerusalem to be consecrated. The law actually stipulated a year old lamb as the required sacrifice [Lev. 12: 6] and a young pigeon or dove for a sin offering. Leviticus 12: 8 goes on to say, "If she cannot afford a lamb, she is to bring two doves or two young pigeons"- this was Mary's offering. If you had any doubt, this confirms that Jesus was born into very humble circumstances.

- As silent as God's voice may have been to the nation of Israel those 400 years since the O.T., God continued to speak to those who were willing to listen, or maybe it was to those who were willing to pay the price to hear. Simeon had a heart longing for the Lord [vs. 25] and the Lord had revealed to him that he would see Messiah before he died [vs.26]. So all-encompassing was this desire that upon taking Jesus in his arms he could then say to God *"Tek mi nou"* ([You can] take me now) - this world had nothing to hold him. His one desire had been to see the Christ. How many of us can say that?

- It blesses me that the prophetess Anna was mentioned, being a woman myself. She "worshipped night and day, fasting and praying" and so was in a position to hear God speak. Simeon and Anna demonstrate a foreshadowing of what Joel prophesied in Joel 2: 28- 29:

"And afterward, I will pour out My Spirit on all people. Your sons and daughters will prophesy, your old men will dream dreams; your young men will see visions. Even on my servants, both men and women, I will pour out My Spirit in those days."

Does anything strike you from Simeon's prophecy? _____
_____
_____

He declared that this "salvation" was "in the sight of ALL people"- so though the Jews looked for it, it was meant for all- Jews and Gentile; and he further declared, by the Holy Spirit that Jesus was a light for revelation to the Gentiles. This must have been under the inspiration of the Holy Spirit because Jews in general didn't consider the Gentiles to be included in the redemption by Messiah. After all, Messiah was coming as King and ruler, to free Israel from the domination of their Gentile masters and to return it to its sovereign state where they, the Jews, ruled themselves. By the Spirit Simeon saw way beyond that … to what Jesus really came to usher in, even though this would not come to pass until sometime after Jesus' death and resurrection.

If you were Mary, what would you have thought of the words Simeon said over your child? [vs. 34 – 35] _____
_____

It must have been encouraging and overwhelming to Mary and Joseph to have not one but two prophetic utterances confirming what God had already said over nine months ago- have no doubt about it, this is the Christ. I wonder what the hearers thought and did- all those fortunate enough to have been in the temple that day? Verse 36 said Anna spoke about Jesus to those who had been watching for Messiah- surely she was declaring *"Si im ya!"* (See, He's here!).

READ MATTHEW 2: 1 – 23
What fresh insights do you pick up? _____
_____
_____
_____

Many a Christmas story leave us with a picture of Jesus lying in a feeding trough, surrounded by diverse farm animals with wise men (Magi/

Kings) in their majestic robes on their knees in the humble cramped surroundings of a stable shortly after Jesus' birth. Given that they could read and understand the stars, it is likely that they were astrologers, not kings. We do not know how many Magi came to worship Jesus and, from verse 11, they did not arrive on the day of His birth and visit Him in the stable but rather came to the house where Jesus and His family were staying. It is likely that once the rush to find a place for Mary to deliver her baby had passed and they had rested, proper lodgings were subsequently found.

King Herod was not Jewish. He was an Idumean appointed King of Judea by Rome. The fact that the Magi came from the East and asked for the King of the Jews meant they were Gentiles. King Herod would clearly be upset to hear a child had been *born* king since he was king, but did you notice that verse 3 said "and all Jerusalem with him"? This could not be kept a secret, moreso after the Sadducees and teachers of the law (the leaders in the Jewish community) had to be called in to explain where, according to the Scriptures, Messiah was to be born. Rumours must have been abounding that Messiah was born ... but they couldn't find Him ...only the ones who were seeking Him to worship Him. So it is today, it is when we seek Him with all our hearts – truly longing to know Him and obey Him- that we will find Him.

The quote in Matt. 2: 6 comes from Micah 5:2 and actually says,"...out of you will come for me one who will be ruler over Israel, *whose origins are from of old, from ancient times (or days of eternity)*" and here demonstrates that Jesus was indeed God (existing from eternity past) made flesh.

Mary must have been overwhelmed- the surprises just never seemed to end. Verse 12 illustrates that seeking hearts are guided by the Lord. Like every father, God ensures the protection of His infant Son, guiding Joseph to escape to Egypt. Herod, having been outsmarted by the Magi, realized he couldn't pinpoint the exact time of Jesus' birth- Jesus could have been anywhere from a few months old to a few years old. We know that certainly He was over 1 ½ months since Luke told us He had been circumcised and consecrated and, given that Joseph fled with his family to Egypt shortly after the Magi's visit, those events must have occurred prior to their visit. Herod died in 4 BC and it was after this that Joseph and his family left Egypt. This means that Jesus spent His infancy in Egypt, but we do not know exactly how long.

Matthew quotes the prophet Hosea [11: 1] in verse 15,"Out of Egypt I called my son". There, the prophet Hosea was actually referring to Israel but it is here applied to Jesus. This is because Jesus was also actually taking on the role of Israel. Note some correlations: Jesus is taken to Egypt to preserve His life, just as Israel (Jacob and his entire family) went to Egypt during the famine to ensure their survival [Gen. 41 – 46]. Likewise, Moses led Israel from slavery out of Egypt and God declared that Israel was to be for Him a kingdom of priests- set apart and distinct from the surrounding nations to show forth the praises of God. Jesus was brought out of Egypt and would go on to succeed where Israel failed. He would "replace" them, succeeding where they failed and bringing redemption in the process.

Finally, we see the young family moving to an obscure town- Nazareth- and here is where Jesus grew up.

So thus far we see Jesus being born in Bethlehem, taken to Jerusalem when He was 40 days old to be consecrated, returning to Bethlehem where the Magi came and offered gifts and worshipped Him, fleeing to Egypt to escape Herod's plan to kill Him, then returning and settling in Nazareth in Galilee. The last glimpse we have into His childhood is recorded in –

LUKE 2: 41 – 52 … PLEASE READ.
What are the revelations that you received as you reflected on this passage?
_____
_____
_____
_____

Verse 41 implies that His parents had obedient hearts desiring to do God's will- going every year to Jerusalem to Passover. Jesus was now 12 years old, poised to enter manhood. We may be tempted to berate Joseph and Mary as being careless and irresponsible parents- I mean, really, how could you **not** know that He wasn't there ... and for a whole day! But really, it was the custom for the extended family and even friends to travel together- each with their own families. Therefore, it would have been a large retinue. By now, Joseph and Mary would have had other children and Jesus was old enough to likely be playing with the other children His own age. It was not farfetched to assume He was among their relatives or friends ... but how many times have *we* been guilty of being so busy and preoccupied that we don't have the time to spend with Jesus and we just assume that He is still with us?

When I add up the day's travel from Jerusalem, another day to return to look for Him plus *three days* of searching- being a parent myself, I can feel the increasing panic and fear in Jesus' parents as they search this large city for their first born. Imagine their thoughts... what would cross your mind?

Oh, the relief at seeing Him, safe and sound (and completely unperturbed!) among the teachers in the temple. I don't doubt that just as we will see later in His discourses and lessons to the Pharisees and others, even at 12, He was showing them new insights into the Scriptures- leaving all who heard Him amazed and astonished. Reflect on His response to His mother's anxious query.

Do you realize that Jesus was calmly sitting in the temple because He believed that there was the most natural place to be and therefore the first place that His parents should have looked for Him- in His Father's house and about His Father's business! I believe Luke recorded this so we could see that even at this young age, Jesus already had an idea of His mission here on earth. Do not miss verse 51. Even though He knew He had been sent from the Father and here for a purpose, He *submitted* and was obedient to His earthly parents *waiting for God's timing to move out into His ministry*. Many times we know and understand that God is calling us to a particular ministry or area of service but we rush ahead of His timing, refusing to remain in submission to the authority

He has placed over us- whether parents, teachers, pastors or spiritual leaders- not allowing the Spirit to mature us and fully equip us for that mission. Remember this- Joseph, Samuel, David and even Jesus, Himself- submitted and waited. What was said of Jesus in verse 52 reflects what was said of Samuel in 1 Sam. 2: 26.

BRINGING IT HOME: -

Pause now for a moment and reflect- what is your response to this Jesus?
Is it adoration and awe like the shepherds, or have you no room for Him?
Is it longing for Him like Simeon and Anna?
Is it submission and worship like the Magi and the herald angels?
Is it rejection like King Herod? ...or
Are you traveling along this life, assuming He is with you, but have left Him behind?
For the Christian- are you, like Jesus, about your Father's business?
For the non-Christian who is not walking with Him, I urge you to bow before Him and accept this precious gift into your heart, making Him Saviour and Lord of your life.

PRAYER: -

Lord Jesus, I confess that I am a sinner- trying to live a good life but, on my own, failing miserably. Please, Lord, forgive my sinful, self-willed and rebellious way of life, and wash me clean. Jesus, I receive You now personally, as my Saviour and Lord, and submit to You completely. Change me. Reveal Yourself in me and make me new. Help me by your Holy Spirit to walk in obedience to Your Word and Your way. Thank You Jesus for saving me from eternal death, buying me back with Your blood and allowing me to be declared not guilty by God. Thank You for this new beginning. Hallelujah!

CHAPTER 6
SON OF MAN

Thus far we have looked at all the Bible records regarding Jesus' infancy and childhood. We now skip approximately eighteen years [Luke 3: 23a] as we look at Him moving out into His ministry.

READ LUKE 3: 1 – 18 and MATTHEW 3: 4 – 5; then MATTHEW 3: 13 – 17
Why do you think these records were included in the gospel? _____
_____
_____
_____

What have you learned about-
   John the Baptist _____
   His followers _____
   Jesus? _____

I initially chose Luke's account because Luke, the consummate historian, takes pains to establish the historical period. It highlights for me the accuracy and truth of the account. I wonder if you have the same picture of John as I have in my mind. Notice he was living in the desert [Luke 3: 2] and wore simple clothes- (made of camel hair and girded at the waist with a leather belt) and ate only what the desert provided- locusts (yuck!) and wild honey. Imagine him with long unruly hair, a long beard, sun-scorched and rugged. I wonder how many of us would have listened to him now, or would we have dismissed him as indigent, or a madman!

Nevertheless, he had the attention of the people- even some of the Pharisees and Sadducees. Matthew's gospel records the insults he gave ("brood of vipers") as being levied at these teachers of the law, rather than at the crowds. Either way, he served to wake Israel up from its slumber and complacency- it was *not* business as usual- share with those in need, don't extort money or be dishonest, be content. Don't just say you have repented; demonstrate it by the way you live your life ("produce fruit in keeping with repentance"). Stop thinking you are safe just because you belong to God's chosen people (Abraham's seed) – that won't save you.

He was also careful to point the people to Messiah [verses 16- 17], warning that judgment was near. Prepare the way he did, indeed.

What do you think Jesus meant in Matt. 3: 15 when He said, "to fulfill all righteousness"?_____

_____

What distinction do you think is there between the baptism for repentance and that with the Holy Spirit and with fire? _____

_____

_____

The word baptize comes from the Greek word "baptizo" which means to immerse, dip or bury. This comes from a term used in reference to immersing a garment first into bleach and then into dye, thus whitening, then changing the colour of the material. You can see the comparison to cleansing from sin and becoming a new creature. You can understand then why John would hesitate to baptize Jesus- since He was without sin. However, Jesus knew He came as the "scapegoat", the representative of Israel **and** indeed of the whole human race; and by being baptized, He was identifying Himself with our sin. It also served to demonstrate that He was consecrated to God and, with the Spirit of God lighting on Him, declared God's approval. It was a confirmation for John that He, Jesus, was indeed the Messiah. It almost seems like a baton or mantle was passed on, in the sense that shortly after this meeting between the two, John was imprisoned and Jesus began His earthly ministry.

This baptism was a baptism of repentance- turning away from sin. After Jesus was crucified, buried and resurrected, only then was the way paved for the Holy Spirit to infill all who would appropriate that sacrifice- those who would turn away from sin, and toward the Saviour, being empowered by the Holy Spirit.

READ LUKE 4: 1 – 13

Have you noticed that a mountain top experience always seems to be followed by the valley of testing? For Jesus it was no different. What do you notice here about this experience?_____

_____

_____

_____

Notice that Jesus was **led** by the Spirit into the desert- a reflection of Israel being led into the wilderness after their deliverance from Pharaoh in Egypt, being "baptized" as they passed through the Red Sea. Recall in Chapter 5 we said that Jesus was taking on the role of Israel, succeeding where they failed. So we can now see the correlations- Israel wandered 40 years in the wilderness, Jesus spent 40 days and 40 nights in the wilderness. In **Deuteronomy 8: 2 – 3**, Moses declared to the Israelites:

> *"Remember how the Lord your God led you all the way in the desert these forty years; to humble you and to test you in order to know what was in your heart, whether or not you would keep His commands. He humbled you, causing you to hunger and then feeding you with manna, which neither you nor your fathers had known, to teach you that man does not live on bread alone but on every word that comes from the mouth of the Lord." (Memory verse)*

The temptations the children of Israel experienced in the desert were to test and to teach them, exposing their hearts and developing trust in God.

Here in Luke, verse 2 tells us Jesus was tempted by the devil throughout the 40 days. I don't think it is a coincidence that Jesus quoted this very same verse from Deuteronomy. He was "Tempted in every way, just as we are- yet was without sin". He succeeded where Israel failed and He also came to show **us** the way. He came to represent **all** mankind and because He underwent the same temptations we go through, He is the perfect High Priest- able to identify with us.

How did Jesus respond to the devil's temptations? _____

I do not want us to so deify Jesus that we miss the very human context of these temptations. Have you ever felt certain that God is calling you to a particular area of ministry? Maybe even others have confirmed the gift in you. Though you recognize the call, and are willing to walk out in God's purpose for you, there is some measure of anxiety as you wonder if you are able to do it. Then the devil comes along and starts planting doubts in your mind, especially if you should make a mistake… "How come you claim to be a worship leader (bible teacher/ evangelist) and you can't even speak clearly in front of a microphone?"… "Did God really call you, or did you just dream that up?" … "If God really did, then tell the pastor to make you preach instead of ……"

This was the devil's ploy. He came along and whispered to Jesus, "Are You really the Son of God? Well if You are, prove it- so everyone will know and there will be no question about it!" Jesus could have done so- He could have unleashed a demonstration of His Godly powers; or He could have, by His Word disposed of Satan and rid us all of the trouble. But He didn't. Jesus knew exactly who He was and felt no need to prove it; God had already said it at His baptism. I believe Jesus' response to the devil shows us how to respond when he comes and attacks. He didn't get into any argument or philosophical discussion with him. He quoted the Word of God… that TRUTH withstands any and all of Satan's lies and deceptions. And that Word is available to us as well- it is our Sword of the Spirit.

The three temptations recorded also coincide with the "things of this world" listed in 1 John 2: 15 – 17:

1. The lust of the flesh (needs)/ cravings of sinful man
2. The lust of the eyes (desires)
3. The pride of life (ego/pride)/ boasting

1 John says they "come not from the Father but from the world".

What did you think about verse 6 in Luke 4? Was Satan lying about having the authority of all the kingdoms of the world? I notice Jesus never confronted him on that. _____

_____

_____

John 12: 31 and 14: 30 describe the devil as the "prince of this world" (connoting rulership) and 1 John 5: 19 acknowledges that "the whole world is under the control of the evil one", but in the end Revelation 11: 15 declares, "The kingdom (many versions say "kingdoms") of the world has become the kingdom of our Lord and of His Christ, and He will reign forever and ever". Hallelujah!

Yes, Satan may know the Holy Scriptures but, like Jesus, we can use the sword of the Spirit i.e. the Word of God and defeat him. He knows his time is short [Rev. 12: 12] and by the blood of Jesus, we are victorious! Let us keep up our guard. Notice Luke 4: 13 – the devil left Jesus *until an opportune time*- he keeps on trying.

PRAYER: -
Father, Your word declares that "His divine power has given us everything we need for life and godliness". Lord, teach me and show me how to apply Your word to my daily life and to use that word rightly in the face of temptations and attacks from the enemy. Thank You for the victory I have in You.

CHAPTER 7
THE DISCIPLES

By now you may have realized that we have been attempting to, as far as possible, lay down the sequence of events as they occurred in Christ's life- a history ("His- story"), so to speak. Along the way, we get to clarify what may appear at a glance to be conflicts or contradictions, as well as get the opportunity to walk with Him; to understand His ways and to identify more with those He encountered. There is a Jamaican saying, *"Si mi an kom liv wid mi…"* which essentially is saying, "Seeing me is one thing, but when you come and live with me…then you really get to know me." My prayer is that as we walk with Jesus through this study of His time here on earth, we would *"kom liv wid"* Him.

One area that may appear to be contradictory when we read the four gospels is the calling of Jesus' first disciples. Come now with me as we examine these eye-witness accounts and clarify what really happened as well as identify just who were these disciples. Remember these were the ones who knew Him most intimately. We will see who they were when Jesus called them, and who they become as they experience the transforming work of the Son of God. In fact we'll come face to face with their humanity and realize that really, they were no different from you and me. We tend to envision them as these super-spiritual "heroes of the faith" but as we journey with them and with Jesus through this study, we come to recognize ourselves in them- fears, agendas, failings and all… but still loved and accepted by Him.

READ JOHN 1: 29 – 51, then look at MARK 1: 14 – 20 & LUKE 5: 1 – 11
What do you glean from these passages? _____

_____

_____

_____

At first glance you might think that somebody got their story mixed up
but let us look closely.

In the Apostle John's account, John the Baptist has not yet been imprisoned
by Herod (c.f. Luke 3: 19 – 20). John the Baptist had received confirmation
that Jesus is the Christ when the Spirit rested on Him following His
baptism. John believes, and his response to believing was to testify- so
he does just that to two of his own followers, Andrew [John 1: 40] and
another unnamed disciple. These two spend the rest of that day with
Jesus. Andrew clearly believed and testified to his brother Simon (later
named Peter by Jesus) whom he brings to meet Jesus. At this point it
does not appear that Jesus is actively ministering nor does it say that
they left everything and followed Jesus. Remember, John the Baptist is
still free. Jesus **does** call Philip who later brings Nathanael to meet Him.
Nathanael, a skeptic initially, believes after Jesus tells him a word of
Knowledge concerning himself. I wonder if he was embarrassed about
his comment when Jesus told him He had seen him before Philip called
him ("Can anything good come from Nazareth?").

Mark's gospel points out in 1: 14 that it was **after** John was imprisoned
that Jesus started preaching and **then** called Peter, Andrew and the sons
of Zebedee (James and John). In fact Matt. 4: 12 – 17 point out that Jesus
left Nazareth and went to live in Capernaum, and it was from there that
He started His ministry. Luke's account gives us the details of the call of
these four fishermen.

Given this synopsis, what do you make of Simon Peter's actions in the
account in Luke? _____

_____

_____

I believe Simon heard his brother's testimony about Jesus but "filed it away" for further thought. He was not yet convinced. Yes, Peter respected Him as a teacher and a good man, affording Him the use of His boat to teach and even putting back out to sea to facilitate Him (though Peter must have been really tired having worked hard all night [vs. 5]). I think up to this point, Peter likely **wanted** to believe Jesus was Messiah, letting down his nets at His command, despite thinking it would be futile. The results shattered his doubts. He had come face to face with the Lord; an encounter so real that Peter could see the sinfulness of himself... he was so unworthy! Like others before him, and since, an encounter with Jesus opened his eyes to his lack. He could not stand in the presence of this Holy God.

What about you? Have you had an encounter with Jesus?

Jesus' presence changes your reality. What was impossible becomes possible... but not only does He change your circumstances, He changes you. It leaves you with no other valid choice than to follow Him- to surrender your life to Him. You are His, for His use and purpose... and so four fishermen left all they knew and followed Him.

What glimpses do you get into the characters or attitudes of the disciples mentioned so far? _____

_____

_____

_____

In summary, John the Baptist pointed his disciples to Jesus and they got to know Him, but Jesus did not call them to active discipleship until after John was imprisoned. After John completed his mission given by God- he prepared the way- then Jesus took over, preaching the message of salvation.

Though there were other disciples, the calling of only one other was also emphasized in the gospels. Levi joined the group sometime after Jesus began ministering.

READ and compare: LUKE 5: 27 – 32, MATT. 9: 9 – 13 & MARK 2: 13 – 17
What information is given in these verses? _____

_____

_____

Why do you think Levi's calling was also singled out? _____

_____

From these three accounts, we discover that

- Matthew was also called Levi
- He was a tax collector
- His father was Alphaeus
- Tax collectors were looked down upon and considered among the sinners in the Jewish community
- Jesus came for sinners and He calls them too!

Tax collectors were one group that was particularly shunned in the Jewish community because they were perceived as traitors, collecting money from their own kind to give to the Roman authorities. Worse, many of them were corrupt and dishonest, collecting more than required, feathering their own nest. [Recall John the Baptist charging them to stop doing so in Luke 3: 12 – 13]. The Pharisees were disgusted when they saw Jesus associating with them; after all, He was supposed to be a great moral teacher.

What do you think Jesus was getting at in His response to them in Matt. 9: 13? _____

_____

This quote comes from Hosea 6: 6 where the Lord, through the prophet, was rebuking Israel because their love was not truly from their heart but just an external carrying out of what they believed God's law required… so they offered sacrifices for their sins and thought that this outward show of worship was sufficient to make them right with God but their hearts never truly turned to Him. The word "mercy" there is translated from the Hebrew word "hesed" which speaks to a steadfast, loyal and covenant- keeping love. Thus, this was really a rebuke to the Pharisees who had their priorities reversed as they ensured that appearances were right while their hearts remained like stone. These "sinners" were closer to God because they were acknowledging Jesus while the teachers of the law were focused on Jesus keeping up with their standard of purity. Jesus was essentially saying that the ones whose hearts are turned to Him, those are the ones that God desires.

Do you get it? Your background, your past life, your family and all your mistakes do not disqualify you as long as your heart is yielded to Him... come just as you are! Do not let what others think of you hinder or prevent you from laying hold of this prize- that of having the privilege of following Him. Are you still waiting? "It is not the healthy who need a doctor, but the sick."

The names of the twelve disciples/apostles are given in the three synoptic gospels and in Acts [Matt. 10: 2 – 4, Mark 3: 16 – 19, Luke 6: 12 – 16 and Acts 1: 13]. Here is a summary: -

NAME	ALSO CALLED	OTHER INFORMATION
Peter	Simon, Cephas	Brothers
Andrew		
John	Sons of Thunder/Sons of Zebedee	Brothers
James		
Philip		
Bartholomew	Likely Nathanael	
Matthew	Levi	Tax Collector
James	Son of Alphaeus/James the Younger	I wonder if he may be a brother of Matthew whose father was also Alphaeus
Thomas	Didymus	
Simon	The Zealot	
Thaddeus	Judas, son of James	
Judas Iscariot		

Peter is always listed first; Judas Iscariot always last. It would be remiss of me, however, to let you believe that these were his only disciples. These may have represented the core group of men, but there were others, and this included a number of significant women... yes, women!

READ LUKE 8: 1 – 3 & LUKE 10: 1
Notice that from verse 3, though some were named, it also said, "and many others". Plus, these women were providing financial support for them (Jesus and his group of followers)... so these were clearly women of means.

READ MARK 15: 40 – 41, MATT. 27: 55 – 56 & ACTS 1: 13 – 15
Again, only a few are named but we are told there were many others. From the account in Acts, we see that they were not just bystanders, but participated in the prayers also. Do not miss the fact that Jesus' brothers are mentioned here. We will look more into that at a later date.

From these accounts, then, we can identify some of the female followers of Jesus:

- Mary Magdalene (mentioned first in the three synoptic gospels and whom Jesus had delivered from seven demons)
- Mary the mother of James the younger (One of the twelve) and Joses
- Salome (possibly the mother of Zebedee's sons, James and John)
- Joanna (the wife of Cuza, the manager of Herod's household – as steward, Cuza would have been responsible for all the wealth and material possessions of Herod, quite a prominent position!), and
- Suzanna (of whom we are told nothing else).

Some believe that James and John may have even been Jesus' cousins. The above passages indicate that it was likely that Salome was their mother. John 19: 25 notes that Jesus' mother Mary, as well as her sister (whom they are suggesting might have been Salome) were near the cross of Jesus at His crucifixion. One other point- let me emphasize that there is NO record of Mary Magdalene being a prostitute!

Jesus called women and did not rebuke or discourage them from following Him or listening to His teaching. In fact, He encouraged it (recall the account of Mary and Martha in Luke 10: 38 – 42). This was revolutionary in a culture that kept women in a lesser 'class'. Jesus came and broke those chains!

So friends, what have we established in our study today?

For me, it demonstrates that God calls ordinary people. People with a questionable past, rich and poor, male and female, labourers and aristocrats, well known and obscure…and those who may have "no claim to fame" i.e. people like you and me.

BRINGING IT HOME: -
Has the Lord been calling you into a particular area of service? What excuses have you been hiding behind? Beloved, He is more than able to equip you and enable you to accomplish that call, while transforming you. Look at where Peter or Mary Magdalene started. Won't you trust Him? Do not let your thoughts and ideas concerning your past, your ability, or your fears hold you back. Jump… He will catch you!

PRAYER: -
Lord, I confess my fears, my doubts, and my inadequacies. I don't know if I can do what You want me to… but I am willing to step out and try, trusting You to be faithful to Your Word. Show me what You desire, Lord, and I will yield. Thank You for even considering me. Have Your way in me, Father.

CHAPTER 8

THE "DEBUT"

⇒ ❋ ⇐

READ JOHN 2: 1 – 11 and write down your impressions.

The account starts off "on the third day"- possibly three days after Jesus decided to leave Bethany (where He had called Philip and Nathanael) for Galilee. There at Cana in Galilee, He along with His mother and disciples attend a wedding. Mary, being a typical woman, shares the concern of the hosts that the wine has run out but, seeing that she comes to Jesus for the solution, it made me stop and think. Her experiences with Him growing up obviously left her with the conviction that He could fix it. Note the endearing respect He holds for her, despite His reluctance. Typical mother- she knows what she knows and will accommodate no argument. It is as if she never heard His resistance- just do it! I have to smile as He submits to her instructions. Many a sermon has been written on this first miracle- I'm sure we have heard different views and many analogies. Right now, though, what I want to point out is that His instructions don't always make sense, at least not to our minds, but oh, the reward when we simply obey and trust.

Of all the things to fix, lack of wine at a party would fall to the bottom of our priority lists- somewhere long after sickness, death, world hunger, even... but fix it He did. Nothing is too small, no need too insignificant- He cares. To summarize:

1. There was a recognition of the need,
2. They asked Him to fix it,

3. They took steps in obedience, and
4. They trusted, even when they didn't understand.

This is a good protocol to follow when we are in a place of needing His intervention- whether it is a sickness, a way-ward child, a failing marriage, or indeed any need. When we acknowledge our lack, and our need for Him and His intervention, we need to be prepared to follow His direction (even when it makes no sense to us). Often our "what makes sense" approaches were getting us nowhere anyway! Do you think you could trust Him with that thing that is so precious to you?

John lets us know this was His first miracle and it served to strengthen the faith of His few new disciples.

READ JOHN 2: 12 – 25.
Compare and contrast with MATT. 21: 12 – 17 & MARK 11: 12 – 18.
Write down your insights.

_____

_____

_____

_____

These accounts appear to be describing two separate incidents. In John's gospel, this event occurs fairly early in Jesus' ministry, while in Matthew and Mark (and Luke), it occurs shortly after His triumphal entry into Jerusalem and shortly before His crucifixion. In John He is coming from Capernaum to Jerusalem, in the synoptics, He came from Jericho, traveling through Bethphage and Bethany. Even what He said and did were sufficiently different (despite some similarities) to convince me that we are looking at two different episodes. Do you agree (don't think that you have to!)?

> **DID YOU KNOW?**
> *"Synoptic" means "see together" and the synoptic gospels comprise Matthew, Mark and Luke. These gospels give a joint view of Jesus Christ, each from their own perspective. As such, we find many similarities between them,*

> *though the emphasis of each one may be different. John's gospel is obviously different from the others. It is believed to be the last one written and seems to supplement the other records. Its style is different; we see him interpreting the events that took place with the aim being to bring those who read it to a saving faith in Jesus Christ [John 20: 31].*

So, early in His ministry, Jesus came to Jerusalem for Passover and was upset when He saw how the temple, His Father's house, was being misused. True, worshippers (especially those traveling from afar) needed to purchase animals for sacrifice and so needed cambio services… but *nat iina di temple itself* (surely not within the temple)! Such practices showed contempt for this holy place and since the chief priests and teachers of the law were not doing anything about it, Jesus took charge. Can you picture it? Cows, sheep and birds out in the temple court… can you smell it? Already, from early in His ministry, we see that He knew where it would take Him [vs. 19 – 21]. Also, His fame was now starting to spread as Jerusalem was exposed to His miracles and many started to believe in Him. Verses 24 – 25 of John chapter 2 let us know that none of this renown went to His head- He knew how fickle mankind could be and so placed no weight on their opinion, adoration and acclaim.

The accounts in the synoptic gospels do not mention cattle and sheep, but even so, they had clearly still not gotten the message… so Jesus points them to the scriptures. Mark gave the more complete quote and if we look back in Isaiah 56 where it comes from, we get a better understanding of what Jesus was driving at.

READ ISAIAH 56: 6 – 7

What do you learn from this? _____

_____

Exactly! Gentiles who desire to worship the Lord were welcome by God to His holy mountain, to His house because He was to be worshipped not only by the Jews but by all people. However, the Jews did not really associate much with Gentiles and the only section of the temple that

Gentiles were allowed to go was in the outer court. Yet, here is exactly where the Jews had transformed into a market-place. Now do you see why Jesus was upset? That is the reason He pointed out that what should be a place of prayer "for all nations" i.e. Gentiles, you have turned into "a den of robbers". This too is a quote from Jeremiah 7: 9 – 11 where God, through the prophet, reprimands Israel for stealing, lying and idolatry while still coming to stand before Him in His temple. In Jesus' time, the merchants were greedy for gain- money was their idol- and they were "worshipping" it right in God's temple.

The children and the "common" people were open to Jesus, not so the chief priests and teachers of the law. Yet it never dawned on them that desiring to kill Him was against God's law- the very thing they purported to stick so rigidly to and demanded of others.

So today, we are exposed to two temperaments of Jesus. In the first instance, He is calm and submissive to His mother, though an adult, while in the clearing of the temple we see Him stern and aggressive. I don't know how anyone can call Him a *maama man* (a wimp). There was no backing down, even when others questioned His authority to do what He did.

What character sketches of Jesus have you made so far?

PRAYER: -
Thank You Lord that You were willing to come down and take on humanity, and experience all the tests and frustrations that we go through daily. Yet You never sinned... and You have instructed us to be holy as You are holy. That must mean that we can be. Help me Lord, to not limit Your work in me. Recognizing my weaknesses, I rejoice in Your strength. Keep me too from sin.

CHAPTER 9
O WHAT A LOVE!

We left off seeing Jesus in Jerusalem becoming famous through the miracles He was performing, though no details were given. He had also caught the attention of the Pharisees and the Sanhedrin (the Jewish ruling council)... how could they ignore Him after the temple clearing episode?! One of their number now comes to Him "to feel Him out".

READ JOHN 3: 1 – 21
What do you learn about Nicodemus? _____
Why do you think Jesus responded to his statement in verse 2 in the way that He did?_____
_____
_____
What did Jesus mean in verse 5 – 8? _____
_____
_____
_____
_____

Nicodemus was not only a Pharisee, but belonged to the Sanhedrin. The Sanhedrin comprised a group of 23 judges appointed in every city of Israel. They were the final authority regarding questions of law.[9] There was also a Great Sanhedrin which was the supreme religious body in the whole land of Israel.[10] This had 71 members in total and comprised elders, teachers of the law and chief priests, including the High Priest.[11] Since this was in Jerusalem and centred around the temple, apparently Nicodemus was a part of the Great Sanhedrin.

Initially, I couldn't understand Jesus' reply to Nicodemus' affirmation that He was a teacher sent from God. As I meditated on it, it seemed to me that Jesus knew what was in Nicodemus' heart so He moved past the preamble and niceties (remember that John chapter 2 ended with Jesus not trusting in man's testimony about Him because He knew that man was fickle), and went straight to the heart of the matter. Nicodemus had come to find out if Jesus was really the Messiah, signaling the long-awaited "kingdom" that the Jews had been looking for- return to self-rule and throwing off Gentile authority. Jesus, knowing this, began to speak of what the kingdom really entailed [vs. 3]. It was essentially a matter of the heart. Nicodemus did not understand, he still had the "world view", so Jesus elaborated in verses 5 and 6.

Let us review what was shared in the Introduction to this study.

READ GENESIS 5: 1 – 3
Do you remember? What did we learn from this?

_____

_____

A major focus of redemption is to recreate the image of God in us. There are many opinions as to what Jesus meant when He said "born of water and the Spirit". Some think it refers to water baptism and baptism in the Holy Spirit. In view of what we just read in Genesis and what verse 6 goes on to say ("flesh gives birth to flesh"), I believe it refers to normal birth and then a spiritual re-birth. In other words, it is a human experience- we alone of all God's creation, angels included, can experience salvation and redemption. So in verses 7 & 8, Jesus tried to get Nicodemus to stop thinking in the physical realm and move his vision to the spiritual context; a spiritual re-birth because the kingdom is not the physical one that Nicodemus was hoping for. As with the wind, you can't see the Spirit but you can see His effect in someone's life [vs. 8]. Therefore it is not something to see with your eyes, it is within you i.e. restoring God's rule within you.

To understand the analogy of Moses and the snake,
READ NUMBERS 21: 4 – 9
What do you notice? _____

_____

The Israelites had refused to enter the Promised Land because of fear and so were condemned by God to roam the desert until they died. Here we find them complaining. Can you believe it, calling the miracle of God's provision, Manna, miserable food?! *Dem aad iez ii?* (Aren't they stubborn and slow to learn?) Please understand that Manna was an O.T. type or foreshadowing of Christ, the bread of life (as we will look at later), so they were rejecting Him when they spoke against it. The Lord punished them for their sin but after they repented, He provided a solution.

Looking at NUM. 21: 8 – 9, what then do you think Jesus meant in JOHN 3: 14 – 15? _____

_____

If Jesus did not come and pay the penalty for our sins, we would have no hope of eternal life. The one who believes in Jesus has eternal life i.e. enters the kingdom of God. Jesus was declaring, "I Am the only access to Heaven".

Have you ever stopped to realize that grumbling is a sin? All that we have- our lives, our health, our jobs, our ability to create wealth, our families, our creative ideas, our food, clothing and shelter- EVERYTHING- comes from God. Paul exhorted the Corinthian church not to grumble as the Israelites did because they were punished for it [1 Corinthians 10: 9 – 10]. He told the Philippians to "do everything without complaining"…"so [they could] become blameless and pure, children of God without fault". Jude in his letter to Christians warned them about godless men who had infiltrated the church. He called them "grumblers and faultfinders" [vs. 16]. In contrast, the writer to the Hebrews urges us to "be content with what you have, because God has said, "Never will I leave you; never will I forsake you"; in fact Hebrews goes on to declare that it is God who will help us so we need not be afraid – *nobadi kyaan du mi notn!* (no-one can trouble me) [vs. 5 & 6]. Paul summed it up nicely in Philip. 4: 11 – 12 when he declared that he had learned to be content, regardless of the circumstances- because the power of Christ within him strengthens and enables him. When we grumble, it is not against people, it is against God because it is He who sovereignly watches over our lives and provides everything for us. Grumbling robs us of our peace. It is sin crouching at our door. When we sin, it is akin to being 'bitten by a snake' i.e. we have served Satan. The solution then for Israel was to look to the symbol of the snake raised up on a pole- but those bitten had to look to it to live. It required belief that such a simple act could save them.

In John's Gospel, Jesus is telling this teacher of the law (Nicodemus) in words he should understand that He, Jesus will also be lifted up on a pole (i.e. crucified) *while bearing all our sin*, in order that those who would "look to the crucified Christ" would live; those "bitten by a snake"- all us sinners- could have eternal life. He expounds on that thought in verse 16. The Bible often interprets itself. If you are wondering how we know what He meant when He said "the Son of Man must be lifted up", John 12: 30 – 33 tells us so. Therefore Jesus' sacrifice and our accepting that sacrifice, made on our behalf, affords us entrance into God's kingdom and a reversal of the sentence of death. It is our hope of eternal life.

Verses 16 and 17 of John chapter 3 hold the most precious and mind-boggling truth of all Scripture. Why would a God who had been rejected and rebelled against do this for such sinners. The amazingly simple answer- because of love! Despite the judgment deserved, He didn't come to condemn, but to retrieve us from sin's clutches… because He loved us **that** much!

I've often wondered if verses 19 & 20 were not a barb at Nicodemus, coming at night to question Jesus. Did he do so just because it was the only time Jesus would be unencumbered by a crowd, or was it out of fear, hoping the crowd would not see him, lest they mistake him for a follower? Yet, don't fret for Nicodemus- look at John 19: 38- 40. What do you learn here?

Yes, I think Nicodemus got it! He believed!

PRAYER: -
What would you like to say to God at this time? Write it here.

CHAPTER 10
A DATE WITH DESTINY

READ JOHN 3: 22 – 36

Could we learn any lessons from this? _____

_____

_____

_____

Look at the argument brought to John the Baptist in verse 26. I wonder if that "certain Jew" [Vs. 25] had incited them by telling them "they weren't doing it right". Regardless, they were clearly offended; after all, "we were here first". How often do pride and our desire to control interfere in the work that God desires to do? God gives us a mission or task, and we become so puffed up over the gift, forgetting it came from Him so there really is nothing to boast about. As a result, *mek enibadi kom chrai fi chienj ou mi aalwiez du it* (no-one had better even attempt to try another way of doing it). We become a hindrance instead of a help. One writer has called offense the bait of Satan. Here, John brings reason and clarity: What we are doing is God's business, it came from Him. Our role is to serve the Christ- let Him have the pre-eminence. If we would only remember this principle in "our" ministries, a great many factions in the church would disappear. John, in humility, had the right attitude- "It's not about me", he says. Again he testified that Jesus was sent by God and reiterated in verse 36 what Jesus had already declared to Nicodemus in John 3: 18.

Now let's turn to one of my favourite passages of Scripture.

READ JOHN 4: 1 – 43

Why do you think the Lord left Judea? _____

What points stand out for you in this discourse?

_____

_____

_____

The gospel writer states that when Jesus learned that the Pharisees had heard that He and His disciples were gaining more followers than John, He left Judea planning to get back to Galilee. I wondered why? Was it because it meant they would now be paying Him too much attention? Was it to make sure that they didn't try to put an end to His ministry prematurely? Did He leave just to be "out of the limelight" for a while?

Notice verse 4 states that He *had* to go through Samaria. This is interesting because Jews generally avoided Samaria and would travel around it; they did not associate with Samaritans [verse 9]. Recall in our Introduction, I pointed out that after King Solomon's death the kingdom of Israel was divided into Northern and Southern kingdoms. The latter called Judah was ruled by the descendants of King David and had Jerusalem as its capital city. The Northern Kingdom became known as Israel and was ruled first by Jeroboam who, in an effort to ensure that the Northern kingdom never reverted back to the House of David, created two golden calves and placed one in Bethel (the southern end of the Northern kingdom) and one in Dan (towards the northern end). This was to prevent the people from having to travel to Jerusalem (the capital of the Southern kingdom) to worship God in His temple, fearing that if they did so, they would again give their allegiance to Rehoboam, King of Judah. One of Jeroboam's successors, Omri, during his reign bought the hill of Samaria from Shemar (1 Kings 16: 23 – 24).It was a strategic defense much like Jerusalem was to Judah and so Samaria became the capital city of the Northern kingdom. In the same way that Jerusalem was often synonymous with the entire Southern kingdom of Judah, so the entire Northern kingdom was often designated Samaria.

Remember also that Samaria/Israel/Northern Kingdom was taken into captivity by Assyria (see Introduction) - this occurred while Hoshea was king of Israel. Shalmaneser, King of Assyria deported the people of Israel to Assyria, and brought in peoples from Babylon as well as other conquered nations into Samaria. The aforementioned mixed worship of God with idol worship [see 2 Kings 17]. They also later intermarried with the remnant of Jews and they and their offspring became known as Samaritans, a race rejected by the Jews.[12] Therefore, although the more direct route from Judea to Galilee was through Samaria, Jesus (like other Jews) could have circumvented Samaria. This means that when the text says that "He had to go through Samaria", it was not that this was geographically necessary. Rather, He had a mission there i.e. it was God's will- a divine appointment.

Part of the reason I love this passage is that it completely upsets the apple cart in terms of what "societal norms" were and how people thought things should be. By the standards of Jesus' time and indeed prior to Him, women were quite marginalized as was evident in their treatment by men. From this account this woman at the well already had three strikes against her: she was female, a Samaritan, and had been divorced so many times plus was now "living in sin". In the eyes of the Jews (including Jesus' disciples and probably even her own people) she was the "dregs" of society; the bottom of the totem pole; "di wat lef" (what remains after everyone has taken what is wanted) - and this is who Jesus had a divine appointment with. She would then be the conduit through which salvation would come to an entire town of people, themselves looked down upon and rejected. It is even more striking because this was still early in Jesus' ministry and yet one of the first groups of people that God sought out for salvation were a mixed race... do you see the significance? Already Jesus was making it evident that He came for *ALL* people, not just the Jews. I love it!

Do you see how patiently and slowly Jesus ministers to her? He starts with where she is at (she has accepted that others reject her) - she herself is taken aback that this Jew would strike up a conversation with her [vs. 9]. Jesus first lifts her vision away from what others think of her to

God- offering her "living water". Some believe this represented eternal life [vs. 14], others think it means the gift of the Holy Spirit [John 7: 38 – 39]. I believe it meant salvation and therefore both of these. She recognizes her hunger, her need [vs. 15]. Then He guides her to her actual state, without condemnation, He simply states the facts. The exposure makes her uncomfortable and she wants to brush past it so she attempts to keep the conversation from getting too personal [vs. 19 & 20]. Jesus brings it home- where you worship is irrelevant, what is important is true worship (from the heart).

What do you think Jesus meant when He said "salvation is from the Jews"? _____

Messiah would come from among the Jewish people… but that did not mean He came only for them. Did you notice that Jesus admitted to this woman that He was indeed the Messiah? I think this is the only place recorded (other than at the trial before His crucifixion) that He states it outright.

Look again at JOHN 4: 27 – 38

1. What do you think the disciples were thinking [vs. 27]?
    _____
    _____

2. What did the woman do? _____

3. What do you understand by verse 32? _____
    _____

4. What was Jesus telling them in verses 34 – 38? _____
    _____
    _____

Now look at verses 39 – 42.

What conclusions can we draw? _____
_____
_____

Just think, one woman –rejected by men- becomes the vessel that brings salvation to a whole town … because the harvest was ripe. The townspeople heard her testimony and were willing to search out the truth for themselves and, because of that, they came to "know that this man really is the Saviour of the world"!

BRINGING IT HOME: -

Have you ever felt offended by the actions of someone else? Was it really because of what they said or did, or because you felt they shouldn't have done what they did? Have you forgiven them?

Is there someone you know who is walking in offense and burdened by unforgiveness? What can you lovingly do to help free them?

Have you felt rejected by others? Have you accepted their labels, or have you opted to walk as Christ sees you? Do you realize you are so special that He would seek you out to draw you to Himself? Yes, you're that special!

PRAYER: -

Lord, I am grateful that You are not limited by society's standards, nor do You desire that we let others limit us. Free me from any feelings of offense or spirit of rejection. Please heal my heart and make me whole. I want to walk in the truth of who I am, as You see me to be. I thank You that there is indeed no condemnation from You. I am free. Teach me too Lord, what it means to worship You in Spirit and in truth. I love You, Lord.

CHAPTER 11
THE NEW COVENANT

Jesus left Samaria after two days [John 4: 43]. It appears that John the Baptist was imprisoned shortly thereafter (we know he was still free before Jesus went to Samaria and had the encounter with the woman at the well). After this happened, Jesus moved to Capernaum [Matt. 4: 12 – 13] and began His ministry in earnest. He called a number of disciples to follow Him (recall chapter 7 of our study), and then went throughout Galilee with His teaching, healing and deliverance ministry- look at MATTHEW 4: 23 – 25. Here we see that people from a wide area were coming to Him, so news about Him was clearly spreading rapidly. Let us look at some of what He taught.

READ MATTHEW 5: 1 – 20

- What strikes you about the Beatitudes? _____
_____
_____
_____

- Why do you think Jesus chose the analogies of salt and light? _____
_____
_____
_____

- What was Jesus getting at in verses 17 – 20? _____
_____
_____

This Sermon on the Mount is the first of five discourses of Jesus that Matthew records. These teachings describe what God really requires of the child of God and were revolutionary when compared to what had always been taught from the Law, in fact this discourse has been considered to be the laying down of the "new law". Jesus by now had a reputation and we find Him being followed by large crowds of people- some seeking healing or deliverance, some wanting understanding, and some just curious.

> **BRAATA: -**
> *Be encouraged to carry out a study on these five discourses of Jesus in Matthew. The others are found in chapters 10, 13, 18, and 24 – 25.*

Chapter 5 of Matthew starts out with Him seeing the crowds and therefore going up the mountainside and sitting down to teach them. Did He do so because it was a good opportunity to spread His doctrine? Or did He see the hunger and need in them and so responded with these revolutionary words of life? Many of them must have felt far from the kingdom, given the rigorous ritualistic standards the teachers of the Law had always espoused. I can almost hear the compassion in His voice as He tells them how it really is…. It is not the haughty and proud ones who will make it, not those who are the influential in this world- that's not what determines one's acceptance by God. Rather, it is the one who recognizes just how lacking and empty he is, how utterly bereft and unworthy, desperately in need of God, having no righteousness in himself, heartbroken over his sin- such a one receives the kingdom. A Kingdom our heavenly Father has great delight in giving! [Luke 12: 32] It is not the ones who look down on others thinking they know the way and are the examples to follow, but the ones who walk in humility, earnestly desiring to follow God's way, demonstrating love by showing mercy to others, walking in truth, and spreading His peace- such are His children. Yes, you may undergo rejection, persecution and even injustice because of Him, but the kingdom of God and your reward in heaven will be certain. No promise of wealth and earthly riches, no high position in society ensured; in fact, just the opposite.

Notice He then switches from speaking about the third person ("blessed are *those*") in verse 10 to speaking to the second person ("blessed are *you*") in verse 11. I believe He moved from addressing His disciples and the crowd in general, and began speaking directly to His close disciples, preparing them from early for the upcoming trials and tests, and reassuring them at the same time. Trouble is going to come to you because of your allegiance to Me, because you will be different, you will be going against the flow, but that's okay- you are to be salt and light. Salt preserves and adds flavour. It makes an impact where it is added and so should you. If you blend in and are no different from the world, then of what use are you? Similarly, even the smallest beam of light dispels darkness. A light that is not shining, that is kept hidden, is also useless. Follow My way and impact your world! God gets the attention and the glory for it.

What He was saying seemed to go against everything the people had been taught by the teachers of the Law, and certainly differed from their example; but Jesus let them know that what He was teaching them was a true understanding of the heart of the Law, not just following the letter of the Law and all the traditions that had been added (as the Pharisees did) [verse 20]. He then goes on to give examples.

READ MATTHEW 5: 21 – 48
- What do you pick up in verse 21? _____
- What is Jesus pointing out in verse 22? _____

    _____

- What about verses 23 and 24? The onus to bring about restitution is on whom? _____
- What stands out as a common thread in all these "new" directives? _

    _____

- Write down any other revelation you gained as you pondered these words:_____

    _____

    _____

    _____

    _____

    _____

Since many modern translations split up each chapter into sections with subheadings, we are often tempted to break the flow of the text, but remember here it was one continuous discourse. Notice Jesus did not say in verse 21 that "The Law said...", rather He said "You have heard that *it was said* to people long ago..." and notice the full statement of just what had been said at that time. Jesus then adds His own "spin". The point I am making is that these instructions flow out of what he had said in verse 20. He said, in effect, *"Ritualistic and rigid observance of the things that you have been taught by the Pharisees and teachers of the law, following their example, will not get you into the kingdom. Living righteously is much more than that. They have told you that you must not murder because anyone who murders will face judgment but God actually is desirous of you knowing the state of your heart before it gets there...don't accept and harbour anger in your heart against your brother. God is looking at the heart before He looks at the actions."*

It seems to me that calling somebody "Raca" (empty-headed) or "a fool" is essentially saying the same thing. In verse 22 therefore, Jesus is effectively telling them that when they sin against their brother in this way, it is not the Sanhedrin they should be afraid of, it is hell-fire! Do you realize how seriously God looks upon such an offense? He is not joking when He says the greatest commandments are love God and love your neighbour!

Hence, verse 23 starts off "Therefore" i.e. it flows out of what He just said in the preceding verses. What is the instruction? Do **whatever it takes** to demonstrate love and be at peace with one another. Notice that it is not that **you** had anything against your brother, but that **he** had something against you. Yet the onus is on **you** to attempt to put it right... **before** you come to worship before God! Then your worship will become acceptable to Him.

In each of the commands that Jesus cited, He first stated what they had been taught then followed it up with a "but" which aimed at getting at what God was really after. Did you notice that He always took it to a higher standard? He described a zero tolerance where sin is concerned. I don't think He expected us to go around eye-less and short of limbs, but was illustrating how seriously and thoroughly we should deal with sin because it will cast us into hell (*a im se so, a no mi* i.e.it was He who said so, not me). In other words, the reality of hell is there in the bible even if we don't want to accept it.

It is not only the woman who is open to being charged with the sin of adultery after a divorce, the same is true for the man.

READ MARK 10: 1 – 12 and MALACHI 2: 13 – 16
What do we learn here? _____
_____
_____

God takes marriages very seriously. I believe Jesus looked and saw some of the situations that the people were involved in, their attitude regarding these things and picked these out to illustrate God's standard. Don't swear by anything because it all belongs to God- don't make Him your guarantor. Demonstrate love and mercy even to those who don't deserve it, even those who hurt you... then you will be imitating your heavenly Father's heart and mind, and how He treats you. Otherwise, what is it that will show you to be different from the unrighteous?

READ MATTHEW 6: 1 – 18
What do you learn about giving? _____ _____ _____
What did Jesus mean when He said, "They have received their reward in full" [vs. 2, 5 & 16]? _____
_____
What was the point Jesus was making when He used the "hypocrites" as an example? _____
What lessons have you learnt about prayer from this passage? _____
_____
_____
_____
_____

How we "practice our Christianity" is not to make us look good in the eyes of men. Rather, it is how God sees us that counts. If what we are doing is just for show, for others to see and honour us, then when they notice us, we have achieved our intention… our reward in full; we accomplished our goal. Don't expect kudos for that in heaven. Based on what Jesus repeatedly said about the Pharisees, this clearly was their usual habit. He did not want the people to be following their bad example. Our giving, and our praying and fasting is about our service and worship to God, not men, so don't seek accolades from men, seek to please God.

Then He taught the right way to pray. I encourage you now to spend some time meditating on it.

What, based on this example of prayer, are the key elements in prayer? _

_____

_____

_____

_____

Note the reverence with which the Father, our Source, is approached. There is firstly the recognition that He stands apart, is distinct and separate; then the invitation, longing and looking for His rule on earth. We are to see Him as the Source for each day's needs. We are to ask for His mercy, even as we extend mercy to each other, while seeking to refrain from sin. One thing I feel compelled to reiterate is the fact that He said to ask God to forgive our sins *as we also forgive those who sin against us*. Then, in case you did not quite get it, He elaborated in verses 14 and 15 that *"if you do not forgive men their sins, your Father will not forgive your sins"*. Yes, that's actually written there in the bible. Stop and think about that!

BRINGING IT HOME: -

When we read these instructions of Jesus, we may feel guilty or even condemned when we realize how far short we fall from God's plan, but this is never the Lord's desire. True, He does not want us to be so comfortable with sin that we make excuses for it, but neither does He want us to feel so past redemption that we give up. There is no thought or action that is outside the cleansing that the blood of

Jesus brings. The word of God says that there is therefore now no condemnation for those who are in Christ Jesus. Repent, confess[naming your sin], forgive and return to God's open arms… "He whom the Son sets free is free indeed".

PRAYER: -

Lord, I hear You calling me to a deeper walk with You. No more can I be satisfied with following the crowd; even the Christian crowd, if they are not living up to Your standards of righteousness. If You say I am to be perfect as You are perfect, it must mean that I can be, or You wouldn't command it. Help me, Lord. Free my mind of the limitations I put upon myself, that hinder You from accomplishing in me all You desire to. Let me be less worried about what others think of me and more concerned with pleasing You. Father, thank You for Your patience and perseverance in transforming me. I love You.

CHAPTER 12

IT'S ALL ABOUT LOVE

Let us continue looking at the instructions in this New Covenant:

READ MATTHEW 6: 19 – 34
What do you understand Him to mean by the word "treasures"? _____
What do you think He meant in verses 22 & 23? _____
_____
_____

Summarize, therefore, His instructions in verses 19 – 24.
_____
_____
_____
_____
_____

What do verses 25 to 34 say to you personally? _____
_____
_____
_____
_____

What does it mean to "seek first His kingdom"? _____
_____
_____
_____

The things that we hold dear and get upset over if they are disturbed, lost or stolen; that which we value highly; that which is precious to us… those are our treasures.

What are some of your treasures?

- o   Home/Vehicle
- o   Job/Salary
- o   Diploma/Degree
- o   Clothes/Jewelry

- o   Spouse/ Personal Relationship
- o   Regard from Others/Reputation
- o   Relationship with God
- o   Other

Jesus admonishes us to hold loosely to the material things- they decay and fade; and can be lost or stolen- such "wealth" is temporary. Rather, make the things that are precious to you be those which assure a reward in the world to come that is eternal. Fix your "eyes" on the things of God. Don't cloud your vision by coveting material and worldly "stuff". They distract you; they make your eyes "bad", putting out the light in you. It is preoccupation with these things that cause us to worry about our needs, forgetting that **God** is our source… not ourselves.

A while back, when I was still single and wondering if I would ever find "the one", some friends and I were doing a bible study on breaking free from all the things that the enemy uses to keep us from being who God called us to be. During that study we looked at this passage of scripture, and we all decided that we were going to focus on seeking after God and the things of God first, expecting Him to keep His word to "add all these things to us"… and I did for a while until the Holy Spirit brought a revelation that was a turning point for me in my walk with God. If our reason for seeking first the things of God was *just so that we would have fulfilled the criteria for getting our heart's desires, then we were not really seeking God first!* Rather, we were still seeking first our heart's desires … because that was our ultimate aim. As my best friend said at the time – she diligently purposed to pray, be faithful in keeping her bible study while keeping in communion with God and living a holy life, and therefore God would see that she could now get her husband. Then God gently pointed out that what she was seeking was the husband, not Him… she was just using Him to get it! What about you my friend- are you seeking after God because you earnestly desire Him and Him alone; or are you hoping that doing so will get your longing fulfilled? God has said He is a jealous God [Exo.34: 14].

Nevertheless, God is faithful- when you are completely sold out to Him and want Him for Himself, you will find all your needs met. In fact, what tends to happen is that you become quite content with who you are and what you have. As another friend would say-"God is just cute that way".

READ MATTHEW 7: 1 – 6
By what standard will you be judged? _____
Rephrase verses 3 – 5 in your own words: _____
_____
_____
What did Jesus mean by what He said in verse 6? _____
_____

Verse 1 implies that we are the ones who determine or set the measuring stick/ standard that will be used when we are judged. If this is so then we should take great care in how we cast judgment on others. Maybe that is exactly what the Lord wants to achieve.

It also makes sense that you examine yourself first. Haven't you ever noticed that when you have stumbled or failed, you have a greater understanding and appreciation of how it feels and therefore demonstrate more compassion for another individual in similar circumstances? You do see more clearly to remove the "speck", and you won't do it by "digging out" your brother's eye (i.e. you will try not to inflict pain and shame on your brother in doing so) - you will instead do so gently.

One of the things I have found also is that one shouldn't try to force the understanding of this principle "down the throat" of others… especially those who still just don't get it. For example, oftentimes we have only a limited knowledge of a situation and though the older or wiser ones try to tell us to be patient and understanding, we disregard the advice, plunge ahead in our self-righteous zeal, and sometimes even curse the advisor... until experience teaches us that they were right. By that time we have left casualties along the way: hurting souls, precious to God, left feeling worthless and condemned. The advice was wasted on us at the time- it was throwing pearls to pigs.

Can you think of other ways that we may "give dogs what is sacred"?

Memory verse: Matthew 7: 1 – 2.

READ MATTHEW 7: 7 – 12
In summary, what is Jesus encouraging us to do? _____

READ LUKE 11: 2 – 13
In that context, what point do you think Jesus is making? _____
_____
Compare Matt. 7: 11 & Luke 11: 13. What is different? _____
_____
Does it make a difference to your understanding of the passage? _____
If so, in what way? _____
What are your thoughts on Matt. 7: 12? _____
_____
_____

Jesus appears to be encouraging us to be bold and persistent in asking of God. The comparative scripture in Luke puts this after His teaching on how to pray. Taken in that context, with the subsequent example of a man disturbing his neighbor late at night but getting what he requested; leads me to the conclusion that Jesus is assuring us that our prayers will be answered, so persevere in asking! In fact, the implication is that our prayers will be answered *because* we persevere, as this indicates our trust and complete dependence on God. We can trust God that He will give good things to us, not things that will harm us- if our friends don't treat us that way, why do we expect God to do so? The fact that Jesus said God would give the Holy Spirit to those who ask Him in Luke's version made me stop and think. The Holy Spirit is God's deposit in us, sealing us as

His own and guaranteeing our inheritance. He is the surety that all that is God's is ours… we are His heirs. Every spiritual blessing in Christ is ours through the Holy Spirit. I believe that Jesus is saying that all of heaven's resources are at our disposal…it is ours for the asking. The Holy Spirit also knows the mind of God and so will help us to line up our asking with the perfect will of God for us.

I believe verse 12 summarizes the point of what Jesus has been getting at from He started His teaching of the sermon on the mount…love your neighbour and treat them as you would want to be treated. Notice He says this sums up the Law and the Prophets… in other words, that was God's intention all along, from the very beginning!

READ MATTHEW 7: 13 – 29
What does He mean in verses 13 & 14? _____
_____
How does one recognize a false prophet? _____
How will they come dressed? _____
What does that mean? _____
Who are the only ones who will enter the kingdom of heaven? _____
What were His parting words of assurance? _____
_____

Pardon me as I put it in my own words. *No fala no croud!* (Don't follow the crowd), the way to heaven is the road less travelled. Carefully consider what that means to you in practical terms. The false prophets may appear holy and righteous, the perfect Christian, but their fruit will give them away. I recall when it dawned on me that it is not the people out in the world who are saying "Lord, Lord". No "non-christian" is going to claim the prophetic and work miracles in Jesus' Name. So it means that a lot of "church people" will be in for a shock come judgment day… they could fool all the people, but they cannot fool God. Only the ones who obey Him will be the ones He admits knowing (i.e. having a relationship with).

And so He ends by admonishing His listeners to take heed **and put into practice** what He has taught them, because when the trials come and the going gets tough, they will have a sure foundation. Notice He never promised a bed of roses, expect the storms. The crowds had never been taught like this- He spoke with authority...*a so it go* (that's how it is)!

We have looked at a lot over these last two chapters. I feel we need to take some time to digest and meditate on what we have read and learnt thus far. Does any of what you have read speak directly to circumstances in your life right now? Is the Lord speaking to you through these instructions?

YOUR THOUGHTS: -

PRAYER: -

Lord, I desire to understand your heart and obey your will. Keep me from just carrying out the actions that I think are required of me, rather than having a heart that truly loves You and desires to serve You. Help me to love those around me, even the ones that annoy or upset me. Help me to remember how I would like to be treated and treat others accordingly. Help me, too, Lord, to seek You for You and not for what I think You can give me. Thanks for not treating me the way I really deserve- Your mercy and grace amaze me. Enable me please to put Your Words into practice until they are my very life.

CHAPTER 13
HIS AUTHORITY

The nation of Israel must have been abuzz with the news of Jesus. He was different. He was not afraid to stand up to the Pharisees and teachers of the Law. Not only were His teachings "new" and different, but He demonstrated His power in the healings and deliverance He brought about in the lives of the people.

READ MARK 1: 21 – 34

Where is the setting [vs. 21}? _____

Where was the man who was possessed by an evil spirit? _____

List at least three things that you learn from what the evil spirit said.

_____

_____

_____

What happened in verses 25 & 26?

_____

_____

What was the result?

_____

_____

From verse 29 who went to Simon's home?

_____

What did Jesus heal Simon's mother-in-law of? _____

_____

Look at verse 34. Why do you think He would not let the demons speak?

_____

_____

Now READ MARK 1: 35 – 39

What important insight into Jesus' habits do we garner from this?

_____

_____

READ MARK 1: 40 – 2: 12

What stands out for you when you read the account of the leper?

_____

_____

_____

What do you learn from chapter 2: 1? _____

What was Jesus' first task? _____

What do you think of the actions of the friends of the paralytic?

_____

_____

Why do you think Jesus opted to tell the man his sins were forgiven?

_____

_____

What did that lead to?

_____

_____

If what they said was true, what did that mean? _____

What do you think of Jesus' reply?

_____

_____

_____

The Gospel of Mark is believed to be the first account written as a record of Jesus' life and ministry here on earth. He points out that after Jesus called the first disciples, they went to Capernaum (recall that Matthew had told us He left Nazareth to live in Capernaum after John the Baptist was imprisoned). There He went and taught in the synagogue. It was not lost on me that the possessed man was in the synagogue. There are so many hurting souls needing healing and freedom sitting in our churches every week. For these evil spirits, their number was called! Did you notice that the spirit used the plural "us"? I also noted that they knew exactly who Jesus was and where He came from; and both they and He knew His authority! He spoke and they had to obey... something the teachers of the day never did.

Jesus, the brothers Andrew and Simon (Peter), as well as James and John (the sons of Zebedee) are the ones named going to Simon's home. There He heals Simon's mother-in-law of a fever. By evening the news of what had happened at the synagogue had spread so "the whole town" was gathered at the door, and Jesus responded. I believe He wouldn't let the demons speak and say who He was because He didn't want the people to start a rebellion against Rome, making Him king by force.[13] That was not why He came; though that is the kind of Messiah they were looking for.

Even the Lord Jesus needed to come aside and pray. He did so very early in the morning (and a good thing too since, based on verse 37, *croud a piipl* (a large crowd of people) were already waiting on Him). I believe He needed refreshing for His spirit and He needed direction from His Father. I think this is why, even though the disciples told Him a lot of people were looking for Him, He decided instead to go elsewhere (to the nearby villages). I believe He was following the directions of the Father.

Both in the encounter between Jesus and the Samaritan woman at the well, and here with the leper, I notice that Jesus did not care what people thought. Lepers were considered unclean and therefore they were social outcasts. If you read Leviticus chapter 13, you find a detailed narrative on distinguishing infectious from non-infectious skin diseases. Leviticus 13: 45 & 46 describe the humiliation such an individual was put through. It should be noted that when the bible speaks of leprosy, it is not necessarily denoting the medical condition also called Hansen's Disease, but rather any skin condition considered to be infectious. In the account in Mark, we see Jesus, ignoring the accepted social response to such an afflicted one. He could have just spoken a word as He did on many other occasions, but instead He opted to do much more… He touched him! My heart believes He saw beyond just the affliction to all that came with it- banned from society, abandoned by loved ones, humiliated, rejected and lonely! This stirred His compassion. Human beings thrive on touch. Babies need it to survive. I think even just the touch from Jesus held meaning for this poor man. So unspeakable was his joy that he could not contain it… despite the Lord's instructions. As a result, Jesus had to keep a low profile.

As seems to have been His custom, when the crowds gathered, His first order of business was to preach the word to them. The friends of the paralytic demonstrated a determination in reaching Jesus that I think impressed and pleased Him. In verse 5 we see where Jesus interpreted their **action** as faith; something well pleasing to God. They believed He could fix it and were not going to lose this chance.

I have always wondered why Jesus chose to say that the man's sins were forgiven, rather than "be healed". I notice again that verse 5 states that He said this when He "saw their faith". I wonder if He recognized that they had saving faith, i.e. they believed in Him; or if He felt led to deal with the more eternal needs- forgiveness of sins had eternal implications while disease and disablement ends with this life; or if He wanted to prove a point to the leaders present. Let us not forget that He always sought God's guidance [John 5:19, 7:16, 8:28, 10:38, 12:49]. In the end, the paralytic was healed, and He got the attention of the leaders.

If God alone can forgive sins, and I believe that to be true, then Jesus was telling these teachers of the Law that He indeed was God made manifest- Immanuel, God with us. He was not allowing them to sit on the fence. They were not being given the option of considering Him just some great moral teacher and worker of signs and wonders. Jesus was showing His authority. By His fruit, you would know Him.

Soon after these events, Matthew the tax collector is added to His band of followers. By now Jesus' reputation as a teacher and healer has spread further, and now people were starting to ask Him questions.

READ MARK 2: 18 – 22

What is Jesus telling His enquirers?

_____

_____

_____

_____

I think Jesus was telling them "Don't compare me with others". He is "New Wine"- who He is and what He brings is different from what they have always been taught and what they are used to. Don't try to fit Him in the box of "how it should be" or "how it has always been", or even "how I think it should be"… as it is for new wine that will ferment and expand, the container must be able to accommodate it (new wineskins will expand to accommodate the increase; old wineskins are already stretched and so cannot expand anymore). Jesus "breaks the mold"- don't limit Him to your expectations, the "old wineskins" cannot contain or receive Him.

READ MARK 2: 23 – 3: 15

What lessons do you learn about the Sabbath here?

_____

_____

_____

What do you think Jesus was trying to show them in chapter 3: 4 & 5?

_____

_____

_____

Jesus continued to disturb the status quo. He just would not behave like all the previous leaders the people had known… _an im neva fried a dem iida_ (and He wasn't afraid of them either). The restrictions of the Sabbath had expanded so far beyond what God had intended that keeping to the strict practices (traditions) laid down by the Pharisees superceded caring about the needs of people… and Jesus would have none of it! The Sabbath had been intended to ensure man got the rest he needed ("the Sabbath was made for man"), not to become a millstone around his neck and an excuse to treat your brother uncaringly.

BRINGING IT HOME: -

As we learn from the example of Jesus, pause here a moment and consider. Are you presently restricted by what others think of you or what they expect of you? Does it cause you to compromise on what you really believe? Is this an area of bondage in your life? Ask the Lord if this is so. It is easy to get trapped in the prison of trying to please everybody, fearing that they won't like you if you disagree with them; but as Jesus showed, it is more important to consider what God thinks of you than what others think. If they reject you because you oppose them, that is not a friendship worth keeping. They should love you for who you are... including your opinions. The devil often uses this to silence the voice God has given you by making you feel intimidated and less than you really are. Child of God, walk boldly in the freedom Christ has won for you and do not allow yourself to be bound again by any yoke of slavery. Ask the Lord to reveal to you how He really sees you, and to open your eyes to agreeing with Him that this is who you are- worthy of respect, worthy of receiving and giving love, having an opinion. Then give it in love, not arrogance.

I can still recall the stranglehold the enemy had over me because I wanted people to like me. If something someone did upset me, I had great difficulty even speaking to let them know. I would feel my throat constrict with any attempt to voice my anger, opinion or hurt. It was literally physically impossible. Oddly enough it was a friend who had no such qualms who brought me to tears when she told me in no uncertain terms what she thought of something I had said to her. My typical response to such an occurrence would be to withdraw, build up a nice strong wall around my emotions, tell everybody I am fine when they ask me why I am so quiet, and determine to keep my mouth shut, even if God Himself was directing me to speak. This time, however, the Lord had another plan. Another friend called in the middle of my "melt down" and heard the evidence of my crying in my voice. He dragged from me what had transpired and, I believe by Godly insight, discerned my plan. He quite gently but forcefully asked why I thought my friends would desert me for having an opinion... do I desert them when they voice theirs? It sounds simple, but a light dawned. It led me to seek God to reveal to me what in my past had brought me to that place. God showed me a number of circumstances that had happened in which I opted for the "safe" route of withdrawal and how the enemy had been using that to restrict me- I let him steal my courage. Exposing it, confessing it and rejecting it, I claimed my freedom. Today the person others see is not who I used to be. I am often placed in a position of speaking in front of an audience. I would never have been able to do so if I continued in that place of bondage. Where I used to be very reserved, now I am bold... now I am free!

Jesus walked boldly in the purpose God had laid out for Him. It got Him good attention but it also got Him on the "bad side" of some of the "important" people in the society... but He did not let fear of what they thought of Him (or could do to Him) stop Him. Those He came to help kept coming and they received from Him. We close off today noting that in continuing His mission, He had now reached the place where He selected twelve of His followers, appointing them apostles, having them walk more closely with Him and giving them duties to perform. We see in this a good example to follow in preparing individuals for ministry and leadership. We had already looked at who these 12 were in Chapter 7.

As we look at the timing and process of choosing the 12 apostles, what could we learn about preparing those we believe are called or gifted in any particular area of ministry [Mark 3: 13 – 15]? _____ _____ _

_____ _____ _____ _____ _____ _____

_____ _____ ___ _____ _____ _____

Did you notice that Jesus only did this after having been with these followers for some time? He would have been able to see their characters and personalities in action, and they would have gotten to know what He is like, how He thinks and what He is about. Now He singles out 12 who would "be with Him" [vs.14]- He would mentor and train them more closely, and **then** send them out.

How is the study so far? Are you beginning to get an understanding of who Jesus is- His personality and character, the way He thinks, His heart? Isn't He wonderful?

PRAYER: -

Lord, I thank You that You are not like we are sometimes- hypocritical, selfish, fearful, wavering. I see Your example – Your absolute love for people; Your compassion for those hurting, lonely and in need; Your fearless stand for God's will, despite what others think. Help me to be bold and confident in You; to walk in compassion and love; to speak Your word and hold to its truth, no matter what others say. Free me from being intimidated by others, regardless of who they are, and from keeping silent when You want me to speak. Keep me balanced, however, Lord- not arrogant and unheeding, but walking in wisdom, love and understanding. I thank you that in Jesus I am victorious.

CHAPTER 14

"WHO DO YOU THINK YOU ARE?"

Have you ever received acclaim for something you have done or achieved from a wide cross-section of persons, only to return home to find your closest family and friends are quite unimpressed. Well, it was no different for Jesus. After travelling around preaching and healing, He returned to the place He grew up, Nazareth.

READ LUKE 4: 16 – 30
What activities were listed in this "mission statement"?

_____

_____

_____

What did Jesus mean in verse 21? _____

What is your impression of verses 22 – 27?

_____

_____

_____

> **BRAATA: -**
> Based on your spiritual gifts and abilities, and what those who know you well think is your passion, do you know what your mission is?
> Have you ever sought the Lord about it?

I placed this scripture at this point in our study because, despite the fact that Luke positioned it shortly after Jesus' temptations in the wilderness, in verse 23 Jesus makes reference to the things He had been doing in Capernaum. Therefore, this event must have happened sometime after He went full-force into His ministry (indeed, Matthew mentions it all the way down in Chapter 13), though not necessarily after all that we have discussed in the last few chapters.

The Scripture He read comes from Isaiah 61: 1 – 2. I notice He stopped at proclaiming the year of the Lord's favour, omitting the day of vengeance of our God. Why do you think this is so?

_____

_____

This passage in Isaiah is considered one of those passages in the Old Testament that had an initial, limited fulfillment for the time it was written, but was prophetic for a future age... the Messianic age, during which redemption and salvation would be made available to us. In other words, the Israelites believed that it was speaking to the coming of Messiah. Jesus appropriated what it declared unto Himself, indicating that He was in fact Messiah. I believe He stopped at the point that He did because at this His first coming, He came to bring salvation and deliverance. His second coming will bring judgment (the day of vengeance of our God). Therefore, He ended His reading at the place in the Scripture that was presently fulfilled [vs. 21].

As we read this passage in Luke, I wondered why Jesus seemed to stir up the people by insulting them. After all, from Luke's account, they seemed impressed and "amazed at the gracious words that came from His lips"; even while acknowledging that He was Joseph's son. We get a clearer picture however, when we look at the account in Mark.

READ MARK 6: 1 – 5.
What did the people say when they heard His teaching?

_____

_____

What was their response at the end of it [vs. 3]? _____

What was Jesus' response?_____

_____

What happened as a result? _____

Do you see what offense can do? Both the passages agree that they were impressed with His teachings; they found His words "gracious". It was not **what** He had to say that offended them; it was **who** was saying it... or rather, who **they** knew Him to be. They recognized His wisdom [Mark 6: 2] and power ("He even does miracles"); but despite this evidence they decided *a kudn Mesia* (it couldn't be Messiah). Why? Because *wi nuo im fram im a likl pikni* (we've known Him since He was a little boy); we know His brothers and sisters; He's just a carpenter- He couldn't be **somebody**, and certainly **NOT** Messiah. How dare He even suggest that He is?!

When we turn back to Luke then, Jesus' response in verses 23 – 27 was actually in response to their being offended. Their conclusion about Him choked the Word He presented to them. The consequent lack of faith prevented them from experiencing the power of His healing and deliverance- they missed out on what so many others were experiencing. Only a few sick people were healed. Jesus couldn't believe their lack of faith. Doesn't this remind you of "throwing pearls before pigs"?

Look back at Luke 4.

What do the two examples that Jesus gave in verses 25 – 27 have in common?

_____

_____

What was the lesson in it? _____

Jesus notes that, despite the fact that there were many widows who would have been suffering in Israel during the period of famine in Elijah's time; it was a foreigner that he was sent to- a widow in Zarephath. Likewise, Naaman was not an Israelite but a Syrian. He implied that those closest to these prophets who were living under the covenant of God given through Moses - the Jews - rejected their message, whereas these non-Jews (despised Gentiles living outside of God's covenant) accepted them and therefore actually inherited promises due **only** to those under the Old Covenant, much as was the case for Jesus. It seems to me also that He was being prophetic in that He and His message would be rejected by the Jews and this would lead to the Gentiles being given an opportunity to receive salvation.

READ JOHN 4: 44 – 54

What was the condition of this official's son? _____

_____

Why do you think Jesus made that statement in verse 48? _____

_____

What request did the official make of Jesus? _____
What do you notice about the official's response to Jesus in verse 50? ___

_____

Contrast this with what we just read in Luke 4. _____

_____

_____

Why do you think Jesus opted to heal in this way on this occasion? _____

_____

What was the outcome for the official and his household? _____

_____

Here we find back in Cana in Galilee, close to Nazareth, an official whose son is terminally ill with a high fever. When Jesus seemed to rebuke him by pointing out that "you people" were only interested in seeing miraculous signs and wonders, I wondered why? Was it because as on other occasions He perceived the condition of his heart; or was it because Cana was quite close to Nazareth and may also have been a familiar "stomping ground" for Jesus when He was growing up? Could it be that they also were too familiar with Him to believe that He could be the Messiah? I suspect that this was the reason Luke prefaced this account by pointing out that Jesus had said that a prophet had no honor in his own country [vs. 44]. Therefore, when verse 45 mentions that the Galileans welcomed Him, it appears they just wanted Him to amaze them some more with the miracles He performed, not because they believed in Him.

This official however, unlike the Nazarenes and these other Galileans, refused to take offense. He had a need and was desperate enough to persevere in seeking Jesus' intervention… *"Do, no mek im ded"* ("Please, don't let him die"). I don't know why Jesus chose to "heal from a distance" on this occasion but I wonder if He knew it would have a greater impact on the official and his family. Some commentators do suggest that the official seemed to believe that only Jesus' physical presence would guarantee the child's healing. This seeker would find that Jesus' power spanned even space/distance! Certainly, it changed the heart of the official- he was convinced and convicted- and he and his family were saved.

READ LUKE 7: 1 – 10

Where did this happen? _____

What did the centurion do? _____

_____

What was Jesus response? _____

How does this compare with His response to the official in the previous story? _____

What strikes you about the centurion's actions after? _____

_____

What do you think of Jesus' response? _____

_____

_____

Here we find the scene changes back to Capernaum. As in the case of the official's son, a centurion's valued servant is at death's door. Unlike the situation in Nazareth and Cana where the truth of the saying "Familiarity breeds contempt" was evident, here this man holds Jesus in very high regard. He so completely believes in His power and ability that he doesn't even consider himself worthy of being in the presence of such a One [vs. 7], especially since he is not even a Jew. He asks some Jewish leaders to speak on his behalf and urge Jesus to intervene. Here, Jesus is on His way to do just that when the centurion sends word to ask Him to "just say the word" and he **knows** his servant will be healed… because he understood what authority entailed. In other words, he knew that Jesus had the authority.

When I compare these two records of healing, it appears that Jesus was clearly more impressed with the faith of the centurion ... especially as he was a Gentile. In fact Matthew's account was slightly different, in that it was the centurion himself who came to Jesus with his request but he still said to Jesus that he was not worthy of having Jesus come under his roof. The rest of the account was essentially the same demonstrating the depth of his faith. He believed that Jesus had the authority to just speak the word where He was and the servant would be healed. The account in Matthew however, had one addition.

READ MATTHEW 8: 10 – 13
What comparison did Jesus make here [vs.10]? _____

_____

What was He referring to in verse 11? _____

_____

Who are the subjects of the kingdom? _____
Compare this with Jesus' rebuke in Luke 4: 25 – 27. What thoughts come to mind? _____

_____

_____

_____

Jesus is amazed because nowhere in Israel did He find faith as great as this centurion's (a Gentile). He then looks to the end times after He returns in judgment, at the time of the marriage feast of the Lamb [c.f. Luke 13: 22 – 29 & Revelation 19: 6 – 9]. The subjects of the kingdom are the Jews. Recall in our Introduction I pointed out that at one point in Israel's history, they clamored for a king, not realizing that God Himself was their king. In Deuteronomy 7: 6 we see where God set the people of Israel apart unto Himself. They were His treasured possession, his subjects. I don't believe He meant all Jews would be thrown out of the kingdom, but only those who rejected Him. The point He was making in the passage in Matthew, however, was that "many will come from the east and the west" (the reference in Luke 13 adds north and south) i.e. from all nations- Gentiles (in other words, people like *us*) - who will enter the kingdom ahead of the ones who had a "birthright" so to speak (the Jews), because these Gentiles were believing in Jesus, while the Jews were being skeptical.

Do you believe you are starting to know Jesus a little better now? To understand how He thinks and feels, and how He saw and carried out His mission? From all the accounts we have looked at so far, what are your impressions of Him? If you were to describe Him to someone who had never heard of Him, what would you say? Write it here:

PRAYER: -

Lord, You are so perfect in every way. I see Your compassion always so evident. You were not afraid to stand up for the downtrodden and weak. You always met each person where they were. You never compromised. You were stern with those who needed it, but always and everywhere Your love for humankind was clear. Thank You for Your mercy and Your love. Help me to follow Your example. More and more, let me see You reflected in me. May it draw others to You.

CHAPTER 15
"ARE YOU THE ONE?"

The reactions to Jesus were many and diverse. Each person had to make up his or her own mind about Him. Even John the Baptist, Jesus' forerunner, who by this time had been thrown into prison by Herod, had some hurdles of his own to cross.

READ MATTHEW 11: 2 – 6
Why do you think John sent this question to Jesus? _____
_____
How did Jesus respond? _____
_____
Do you think that was the answer John expected? _____
Why did Jesus respond in this way? What was He showing John? _____
_____

Now, READ MATTHEW 11: 7 – 19
What did Jesus say about John being a prophet? _____
_____
Why is it that anyone who is least in the kingdom of heaven is still greater than John the Baptist? _____
_____
What does He mean by the statement in verse 12? _____
_____
Who does He declare John to be? _____

Discuss what Jesus meant in verses 16 – 19.

_____

_____

_____

_____

_____

Jesus had been ministering for some time now and His Name and activities had spread far and wide. John the Baptist had been in prison all this time. Prior to being incarcerated, he had witnessed and testified to the fact that Jesus was the Messiah. The account in Luke 7: 18 lets us know that John's disciples kept him up to date on what was happening on the "outside". John heard about all the new teaching and the many miracles, even raising someone from the dead [Luke 7: 11 – 17]. Indulge me while I attempt to look into John's mind. Can't you almost hear him questioning? "If He can do all this, if He is Messiah, what is He waiting for to declare it? Why am I still languishing in this place, and unjustly at that? Why doesn't He overthrow Herod and take His throne? What is He waiting for?"

I think John was feeling frustrated and discouraged. How completely human! It is the exposure of such human frailty that helps to confirm in my mind the truth of these accounts. There was no attempt to deny or hide it. The "great" John the Baptist was just as prone to impatience and doubt as the rest of us, even after seeing with his own eyes the Spirit of God descending on Jesus and confirming that He was indeed the Son of God. Just like John, if we don't see our expectations met in the time-frame, and way that we believe it should happen, we get anxious. We start to doubt and question God. Sometimes, like Sarah in Genesis, we go and seek out our own solutions, rather than waiting on God.

Yet Jesus did not give a yes or no answer. Instead He pointed to all the things He had been doing and their effect. As we would say in Jamaica, it was _akshon, nat a bag a mout_ (action, not just talk). More than that, though, I think He was reminding John about what the old testament prophecies had declared Messiah would bring[recall the mission statement quoted by Jesus from Isaiah 61], and in so doing, refocus John's eyes on where they used to be... on God! I don't think Jesus was trying to be difficult; rather I believe He was reassuring this despondent servant of God.

Jesus then addressed the crowd and confirmed that John was indeed a prophet. In fact he was *the* prophet that the Old Testament foretold would precede the Messiah and prepare the way for Him (foretold in Malachi 3: 1 and quoted by Jesus in verse 10). Jesus then made an astounding statement that showed His respect for John. There was no one from the human race greater than John the Baptist...no one born of women. Yet He went on to say anyone who is even the least in the kingdom was greater than John. I believe He was saying that John the Baptist was greater than all who were born in the flesh, but all who were born of the Spirit (i.e. born again, and thus belonging to the kingdom of heaven) were greater than him (John). This is because John would die before Jesus would pay the penalty for our sins and redeem us. We have a greater privilege because we would receive the Holy Spirit and be made joint heirs with Christ. NIV Study Bible puts it nicely- John was only a friend of the bridegroom, we are the bride. John belonged to the old covenant, we belong to the new.

Once John came on the scene, because it heralded the coming of Messiah, it meant it ushered in the kingdom of heaven... the rule of God- and nothing could stop it- it was steadily moving forward and was open to those who were prepared to exercise their will and join it, against the odds(trials, persecution, rejection). Jesus quite clearly stated that John was indeed the "Elijah" that was to come. But there was no pleasing the people: John was somewhat of a recluse, out in the desert, feeding on only what the desert provided. He was not "feasting and partying", and the naysayers had a problem with him for that reason. ["We sang a dirge, and you did not mourn"]. Jesus came and did the opposite- He mixed with the people and ate and drank with them ["we played the flute for you, and you did not dance"], they still had a problem with that. Regardless, the wise ones who accepted their message would be proven right in the end.

BRINGING IT HOME: -

Pause here a moment. Is there anything that speaks to you in this Gospel record that may be relevant to you or your situation now?

Have you been waiting on God for an answer? Does He seem to be taking too long? Did you start out with certainty that God had spoken, but now, after all this time, you are not so sure?

Do you feel like giving up? Are you tempted to turn from the faith? ...Or are you one of the "forceful men" who will lay hold of it?

READ LUKE 7: 36 – 50
Where did this event occur? _____

At what point in Jesus' ministry did this occur? (Choose one)

o   At the start
o   Somewhere in the middle
o   Towards the end

Who was the host of this dinner? _____
What information about the woman is given? _____
What did she do? _____
What was the host's response? _____
_____

Is there anything else that stands out to you in the remainder of this account? _____
_____
_____

Now, compare this to MATTHEW 26: 6 – 13
Look at the passages before and after this record. At what point in Jesus' ministry did this event occur?

o   At the start
o   Somewhere in the middle
o   Towards the end

Where did it happen? _____

What information is given about the host? _____

Who were upset at the woman's actions? _____

What was their concern? _____

What was Jesus' response? _____

_____

_____

READ MARK 14: 1 – 9

What further information is added to the account in Matthew? _____

_____

Now, READ JOHN 12: 1 – 8

What added information about the dinner is given here? _____

_____

Who was the woman? _____

Who raised the objection? _____

What else do we learn about him here? _____

_____

Given all we have read, what can we conclude from all these accounts?

_____

_____

It seems to me that there were two separate episodes involving women pouring expensive perfume on Jesus' head/feet. The record in Luke occurred somewhere in the middle of His ministry, while the other accounts all point to a separate event occurring two days before the final Passover that Jesus would share with His disciples prior to His crucifixion. The earlier event involved a sinful woman, unnamed, who having been forgiven much, loved much. It occurred at Simon (a common Jewish name) the Pharisee's house, and it was the host who had a problem with her display. He was not so much concerned with the cost of the perfume and apparent waste, but moreso with the woman's past and Jesus allowing her to touch Him. Jesus rebuked him because she had done so much more for Jesus, while the Pharisee had apparently not even extended the expected basic common courtesy and hospitality.

The other accounts reflect an event towards the end of Jesus' ministry and, taken together, inform us that a dinner was given in Jesus' honour at the home of Simon the Leper, in Bethany. Lazarus, Mary and Martha (who was also serving) were there; and it was this Mary that anointed Jesus. It appears that Judas Iscariot was the main objector, and though his voiced reason was about helping the poor, apparently an ulterior motive was present. On this occasion, Jesus explained that it was in preparation for His burial.

When I was growing up, I was taught that it was Mary Magdalene, "the prostitute" that did this anointing. We established before that there is no record of her being a prostitute. I suspect this was extrapolated from the "sinful woman" reference. As we now know from our study, it was Mary of Bethany and **not** Mary Magdalene who had done this to Jesus. This is why it is so important to study the bible for ourselves!

So to summarize today's study, we looked at John the Baptist, discouraged, questioning if Jesus really is the One. On the other hand, we see the response of two women whose lives were so touched by the Lord that they had no doubt that He was the One... and so offered up their worship to Him.

PRAYER: -

Lord, teach me how to love as these women loved You- pouring out a costly sacrifice without being asked, recognizing that You deserve so much more. You have forgiven me of so much, and You continue to love me and extend Your mercy towards me. Thank You that even when others do not understand me or would judge me for the things I do, You see my heart and accept my worship, meager though it may be in comparison to what You truly deserve. I love You, Lord.

CHAPTER 16
JUDGE & GIVER OF LIFE

We love to see the unusual and fantastic. New and exciting things draw our attention and make us feel good… for a time. When they become too familiar, or when they challenge us to let go of preconceived or "long-held-unto" habits or ways of thinking; when they go against what we have always held to be true… then the love affair usually ends. The miracles Jesus performed were awesome. The way He spoke and the way He behaved were quite different from what the people had been used to. Now His words and actions were beginning to "rub them the wrong way".

READ JOHN 5: 1 – 15
Is there anything that stands out for you in this passage? _____

_____

How long had this man been an invalid? _____

Why do you think Jesus asked him if he wanted to get well? _____

_____

What was the response of the Jews when they saw the man? _____

The man told them that he had been healed by the one who told him to carry his mat. What was the primary concern of the Jews still? _____

_____

What do you think Jesus meant by what He said in verse 14?

_____

_____

_____

Imagine being an invalid for thirty-eight (38) years, and being within spitting distance of your cure all (or most of) that time. How tragic?! I think this is why Jesus asked him first if he really wanted to be healed. Maybe this was now how he made his living (begging alms) or maybe he had now resigned himself to living this way. Notice that he clearly didn't know who Jesus was; he was not looking to Him to heal him of his disability; but the man did point out the futility of his situation- without help he could not access the miraculous pool at the right time. What an indictment that there had been no-one to help him all those years.

Indeed the callousness of the Jews was still evident when they saw him walking with his mat. If he had been there for 38 years, he would have been easily recognized by the people. Yet, their primary concern was that it was not lawful for him to be carrying his mat on the Sabbath. This, by the way, was not in the Law of Moses, it was added in the Rabbinical traditions. In their zeal to ensure that no work was done on the Sabbath, they swung to the other extreme, having no compassion for those who may be suffering or in need on the Sabbath... let them be healed some other time. No one could find it in their heart to rejoice with this man who was made free after such a long time. They just wanted to find the culprit who had dared to heal him on the Sabbath and then, to make matters worse, compound it by encouraging him to break the Sabbath himself.

Recall in Chapter 13 of our study when we looked at a similar reaction to Jesus when his disciples, being hungry, dared to pick some heads of grain to eat on the Sabbath; and later Jesus healed a man with a shriveled hand in the synagogue on the Sabbath [Mark 2: 23 – 3: 6]. At that time Jesus had declared that "the Son of Man was Lord of the Sabbath" and reiterated that God had instituted the Sabbath for the benefit of man, not his detriment. Again, notice Jesus' heart towards people.

When the man finds Jesus again, Jesus encourages him to stop sinning. After all what is the point of being healthy and whole yet still end up in hell, missing out on being a part of the eternal kingdom.

READ JOHN 5: 16 – 30

What is verse 17 saying? _____

What features of Christ did Jesus list that indicated He was indeed the Messiah? _____

_____

_____

_____

What do you think verse 25 is saying? _____

_____

What do you learn from verses 28 – 30? _____

_____

_____

The Jews were upset that Jesus was, in their view, desecrating the Sabbath and so the persecution started. I cannot ignore His response to them: God is always working, and so is He! Just as God sees each one's needs and fills them, regardless of the day, so Jesus will continue to show compassion to the needy, following in His Father's footsteps. The familiarity with which Jesus spoke about His Father was an affront to the Jews. Note, they recognized that He was making Himself equal with God [vs. 18]... in other words, they knew He was claiming to be Messiah.

But Jesus did not stop there. Aside from calling God His Father intimately, He said He only did what He saw His Father doing, making Himself and God equal in their activity. He said He gives life- something only God could do, and that He is the One who judges- again something only God has the prerogative to do. In these few verses, Jesus was declaring Himself Immanuel, God with us.

I believe Christ was declaring in verse 25 that when the spiritually dead heard His voice and obeyed what He said, they would receive salvation and redemption and so move from being doomed to death, into eternal life. He then moves in verses 28 – 30 to speak of the final judgment when the dead would be raised to face the consequences of the choices they made while alive. Those who rejected Him will rise to be condemned; those who believed in Him will rise to eternal life.

> **BRAATA: -**
> *Revelation 20: 11 – 15 speaks quite clearly to what the end result is of those whose names were not found written in the book of life.*

Memory verse: Revelation 20: 15.

Did you notice that Jesus said that He could do nothing by Himself, that His judgment was based on what He heard from the Father [vs. 30]? He had no hidden agenda; was not *holing up anybady in im art* (had no grudge against anyone) for rejecting Him; was not seeking to please His ego. This is why His judgment was just- He desired to please God and so listened to Him. If Jesus waited to hear from the Father to determine His next move, shouldn't we be doing the same?

READ JOHN 5: 31 – 47

Who are those who will testify on Jesus' behalf?

_____

_____

_____

_____

_____

Jesus proposed that His listeners didn't have to depend upon His affirmations about Himself. There were witnesses who were testifying on His behalf. Therefore, rather than speaking for Himself, He would let these "speak" for Him and the people could judge for themselves whether or not He really was the Messiah. He pointed out that they had already sent to John to find out what he thought of Jesus and John had testified to the truth i.e. confirmed it. Jesus pointed out again that He did not put any weight on human testimony, but was acknowledging it since they thought it so important.

But there was another who testified in His favour [vs. 32] and that testimony held much greater weight... that of the Father Himself [vs. 37]. In fact, the very work that Jesus was doing, by its very nature was declaring that He was Messiah, sent from God [vs. 36]. The Scriptures that they were so diligently studying also testified about Him [vs. 39]. He highlighted their folly- there was so much evidence staring them in the face but still they rejected Him. Yet, if someone else came and proclaimed himself to be the Messiah, they would accept it; so much were they influenced by people which illustrated just how fickle they were. Finally, the patriarch Moses also testified about Him [vs. 46].

But what had Moses said about Him? In our Introduction we already pointed out that when God was declaring curses on Adam, Eve and the serpent, to the serpent He declared that the offspring of the woman would crush his head and he, the serpent, would strike his heel [Genesis 3: 15] - a foreshadowing of the crucifixion of Jesus and the ultimate victory over the serpent in the end when he is cast into the lake of fire. In addition, however, there are other prophecies in the Old Testament (O.T.) and even in the books of Moses (the first five books of the O.T. also called the Pentateuch).

READ GENESIS 49: 10
What do you think was meant when it said "the scepter will not depart from Judah? _____

_____

Who is the passage referring to when it says "until he comes to whom it belongs"? _____

READ EXODUS 12: 1 – 13 & 21 – 23
Who is this a foreshadowing of? _____
[See 1 Corinthians 5:7].

King David was from the tribe of Judah. Even after the Kingdom of Israel was divided, whereas the Northern Kingdom was ruled by kings from different tribes, the line of David was preserved in the Southern Kingdom. Thus, the scepter- the" ruler-ship" of the kingdom – never departed from Judah. Jesus, you will recall, was from the tribe of Judah, of the line of David. He is the One "to whom it belongs".

The institution of the Passover was a reflection and foreshadowing of the work of Jesus Christ. The covenant people of God were spared the judgment of death by the destroying angel because of the blood of the lamb that was painted on their doorposts. That blood marked them as belonging to God and submitted to Him. It was also a foreshadowing of "the blood of the eternal covenant" (Hebrews 13: 20) that He would institute through Jesus' shed blood, and by which we are also sanctified (Hebrew 10:29)! It allowed them to be set free from slavery and to leave Egypt for the Promised Land. Jesus is our Passover Lamb. Those of us who accept His sacrifice have His blood "painted on the doorposts of our lives", so to speak. We are marked as His, and therefore have been set free from slavery to sin and from the concomitant sentence of death. Salvation was determined from the beginning- isn't that awesome?!

These are just two examples of instances in which Moses had effectively written about Messiah. I'm sure there are others, but these suffice to prove Jesus' point that if the people had been less concerned about appearances and what *piipl se* (others were saying), true seekers would have recognized Jesus as the Messiah they had been looking for.

What lessons have we learned to "take home" out of this time in the word?

PRAYER: -
Father, search my heart, now. Where I have become callous and uncaring, more concerned with appearances than with people- please cleanse me, Lord. Forgive me, and restore in me compassion and love, especially for those who are hurting and dispossessed. Grant me Your vision to see people and situations as You see them. Thank You for Your patience Lord.

CHAPTER 17
PRIDE, PETULANCE & PROVISION

We now see Jesus sending out His disciples.

READ MARK 6: 6b – 13
What lessons on discipleship do you learn from this? _____
_____
_____
Is there anything about Jesus' instructions to His disciples that stands out
to you? _____ _____ _____
What were the disciples able to accomplish? _____ _____
_____

Jesus left us a clear example of how to train and disciple believers in the
kingdom. He called them; walked with them, teaching, explaining and
demonstrating; then He anointed and equipped them, sending them out
in pairs, with authority and instruction. In doing so, more "ground was
covered". Do you realize that He essentially instructed them to depend
totally on God to provide for their food and lodging... they were not to
carry any contingencies-WOW! Would you be willing to do that today?
Yet, look at the result of their obedience- all the things that Jesus did, they
were able to do also.

All this while, John the Baptist had been locked away in prison, but more
sinister events had occurred too.

READ MARK 6: 14 – 29

Who did the people believe Jesus to be?

_____

_____

What was missing from these options? _____

Why was John killed? _____

_____

Who are the characters mentioned in this passage?

_____

_____

What do you learn about Herod from this discourse?

_____

_____

What do you learn about Herodias? _____

_____

What do their actions tell you about the state of their heart?

_____

_____

Who would you blame for John's killing and why?

_____

_____

_____

_____

_____

_____

I find this discourse interesting on many levels. I don't recall any record of John the Baptist doing any miracles. In fact, John 10: 41 informs us that he never did. Nevertheless, people were now thinking that Jesus was either John, or Elijah, or some other prophet … never Messiah. Herod's guilty conscience led him to believe that it was the man he had killed- John the Baptist. Notice, Herod had feared John and therefore had refused to have him killed. In fact, the only reason he had imprisoned him in the first place was because his wife Herodias had "made him do it", and this because John had rightly pointed out that it was unlawful for Herod to go and marry his own brother's wife. Herodias had divorced her husband Philip and married Herod Antipas. She held a grudge against John because he told her the truth rather than ignoring it or pretending to agree with it

Both Herod's response to his wife here, and his subsequent behavior in response to the dance of his step-daughter and her request for John's head showed him to be a ruler concerned with what people thought of him, as well as concerned about his ego and pride. Despite his fear of John and his conscience, he imprisoned and subsequently killed John. Because of his rash promises to Herodias' daughter and preoccupation with how he would look in the eyes of his guests, John was beheaded; and clearly since that time, his conscience had been bothering him as he now saw in Jesus the reincarnation of John.

Herodias, like so many of us when we are doing wrong, did not appreciate having her sin pointed out. Yet, rather than repent, she lashed out at the messenger… a common practice today. "Who are you to tell me what to do?"… "Who made you judge?"… And then often all kinds of motives are ascribed to the individual who dared to stand up for God's truth. We become petulant because we want to have our own way, even if it flies in the face of God… and we can find many reasons why God's plan doesn't apply to our situation. The folly here is that she thought that if she removed John from the picture, it would be fine; or maybe it was just extracting revenge. Either way, sin is sin and you can't run away from the truth nor can you cover it up or silence it.

But surely the other dinner guests were just as culpable. These were important people- high officials, military commanders, leading men of Galilee- surely someone could have spoken up for John!

Why allow a man to die as the prize for a dance? By their silence, they aided and abetted in the murder of an innocent man. I wonder if there were others who had wanted him silenced- John had never minced words, he called a spade a spade. Remember he called the Pharisees and Sadducees a "brood of vipers" in Matthew 3 as he was baptizing by the Jordan. I wonder if there were others who held a grudge. Though Herodias' daughter may have made the request and the executioner may have carried out the act, I believe they were the least culpable- they were mere pawns, the latter just carrying out his job.

BRINGING IT HOME: -

You know, it is easy to follow the current practices and ways of thinking, even when it completely goes against the Word of God. Child of God, is there anything you may be guilty of that the world sees nothing wrong with, but you know in your heart that God is displeased? Do you hold a grudge against anyone who may have tried to point out your error? Is there need for repentance... and confession... maybe reconciliation? If your heart is convicted, don't wait. Set things right now!

Now let us return to Jesus.

READ JOHN 6: 1 – 15
Why was the crowd following Jesus? _____
Why do you think Jesus chose to ask Philip? _____
This is the only miracle that Jesus did prior to His resurrection that is recorded in all four gospels.

READ MATTHEW 14: 13 – 14
What was Jesus' response to the crowds? _____

READ MARK 6: 30 – 33 & LUKE 9: 10
What more do we learn here? _____

_____

_____

Looking at all these accounts, what lessons do you learn from Jesus' actions here that may be relevant to us today? _____

_____

What was the response of the crowd at the end? _____
What further information do we learn from Matthew's record in chapter 14: 21? _____

_____

Putting the four accounts together, it appears Jesus had sent out the twelve disciples to continue the works He had started- essentially an apprenticeship. Around that time, John the Baptist was beheaded [Mark 6 & Luke 9]. Jesus heard about this [Matthew 14: 13] and at about the same time the disciples returned and reported their experiences [Mark]. With the crowds always around them, Jesus decided that they needed to withdraw to a solitary place; maybe even allowing them some time to grieve. Luke lets us know they went to the town of Bethsaida [Luke 9: 10]. They did this by boat, crossing the Sea of Galilee (also called the Sea of Tiberias) [John 6: 1].It was a futile effort as many saw them leaving and ran on foot from all the surrounding towns, arriving there before Jesus and His disciples [Mark 6: 33].

I am impressed that, rather than feeling exasperated as so many of us would, Jesus instead felt compassion because He looked past His needs and the needs of His disciples to the needs of the crowd. From Matthew and Mark we learn the disciples became concerned about the lateness of the hour and the remoteness of the place, as it did not provide opportunity for the people to go and find food. Jesus tested Philip by asking him where they could buy food for all these people. It makes sense that He would ask Philip because you will recall Philip, Peter and Andrew were from Bethsaida [John 1: 44], and would therefore be more familiar with the territory and the people. This may also be the reason Andrew was the one who discovered the boy with the loaves and the fish. Rather than pointing out a likely place to eat or buy food, Philip zeroed in on what it would cost... it would simply be impossible! From Mark [vs. 38], we learn that it was Jesus who sent them to find out how many loaves could be collected from the crowd. Imagine, from the crowd of over 5,000 men, only one boy had had the foresight to carry 5 loaves and 2 fish- such had been the haste and urgency of the crowd to see Jesus.

The people were instructed to sit down on the grass in groups and Jesus then did the miraculous. He took the food, offered up thanks to God for it and distributed it to all, until all had enough to eat...so bountiful was the supply, that there were enough leftovers to fill 12 baskets!

What lesson can we learn here?

> *Don't limit God. It might seem like a pittance ("all we have is…"), but offered up in thanksgiving, it will be multiplied to supply the needs of thousands. Nothing is impossible with God. Have you been hiding or refraining from using the gift/ gifts God has given you because they appear so insignificant and inadequate (for the perceived needs). Give thanks for it and let God know it is available for His use.*

Note too that it was *over* 5,000 people who were fed. Matthew lets us know it was 5,000 men *besides* women and children [Matt. 14: 21].

After the people saw the miracle, they began to believe that Jesus may be "the Prophet" who was to come. This is believed to be in reference to Deut. 18: 15.

READ DEUTERONOMY 18: 14 – 22
Who was speaking here? [Refer to the start of the discourse at Deut. 5: 1]

_____

Given the entire context, what do you think was meant in the immediate sense? _____

_____

When we flip back, it becomes evident that Moses was the one speaking here. In fact, all that is written from Chapter 5 through to Chapter 29 of Deuteronomy comprises the Mosaic Law that was laid down for the people of Israel prior to the death of Moses – Deut. 4: 44 – 49 introduces that law. When we read through Chapter 18, however, it becomes evident that Moses was referring to: a) his immediate successor- a prophet God would raise up that would continue to lead the people after Moses' death and b) others who would in the future be called to lead the people. However, recall we had pointed out before that a lot of the prophecies of the Old Testament had an immediate **and** a future fulfillment. The Israelites believed that though this did refer to the subsequent prophets that God would raise up to lead His people, it would eventually find its ultimate fulfillment in the coming of Messiah, who would come "from among [their] own brothers".

Returning to the passage in John 6, when the people saw how Jesus had miraculously provided food for over 5,000 people, they believed He may very well be that "Prophet" i.e. Messiah- the One who would be raised up by God to lead His people. They were ready to make Him King of the Jews by force, and throw off Roman rule. Jesus knew that, though He was Messiah, it was not that Kingdom He had come to advance.

Well, we certainly have looked at a lot this session. What are some of the things that made an impact on you (i.e. were relevant to you and your circumstances)? Write them here: -

What did you learn about following the call of God on your life when you look at the way John died?

What "snapshots" of i) Jesus, and ii) His disciples did you get in the account of the feeding of the 5,000?

Did they mean anything to you as a disciple/follower of Jesus yourself?

PRAYER: -

Lord, it seems so unfair sometimes. I have decided to follow You, no matter the cost, but sometimes it is so hard. Yet as I look on the lives of Your servants, they were just as human and prone to fear, discouragement and disbelief as I am. John died without justice, even though Jesus was walking the earth at the time. Help me to press on even when I can't see You. Help me to not follow the world, but rather Your Word. Help me be faithful to the end.

CHAPTER 18
THE BREAD OF LIFE

We ended the previous chapter with Jesus withdrawing from the crowd and going to the mountainside by Himself.

READ JOHN 6: 16 – 24, then compare to MATTHEW 14: 22 – 33
We read previously that Jesus had recognized that the people wanted to make Him King by force. From these two accounts today,

1. What did Jesus subsequently do? [Matt. 14: 22]

    _____

    _____

2. Why did He go up the mountain? _____

Read a section of Mark's recollection in MARK 6: 47 – 49.

3. What time was it when the boat reached the middle of the lake? ____
4. What did Jesus notice then? _____
5. What time was it when Jesus went out to the disciples? _____

Looking back at the account in Matthew:

6. Why did Peter start to sink? _____

    _____

7. What was his next action? _____

8. What happened as a result? _____
9. What did Jesus say was the reason Peter began to sink? _____
10. What happened when they got into the boat? _____
11. What, according to John's account, happened when Jesus got into the boat?_____
    _____

12. What did the crowd who had been left behind do when they could not find Jesus and His disciples? _____
13. When Jesus arrived in Gennesaret, what happened? _____
    _____
    _____
    _____
    _____

14. Taking all the accounts together, are there any lessons that you could learn that could guide you in any present or future circumstance?
    _____
    _____

I took note of the fact that when Jesus understood that the people wanted to make Him king, not only did He send them away; he also had His disciples go on ahead of Him.

LESSON 1: Even Jesus needed some alone time to pray and connect with His Father, especially after a time of intense ministry… how much more us mere mortals. Pastors, leaders, worship team and all Christians actively walking in the calling God has placed upon you- take note!

The accounts make note of the fact that the disciples had made it as far as the middle of the lake by evening. Mark then lets us know that Jesus saw them struggling against the wind. Yet, it wasn't until the fourth watch of the night (between 3 am and 6 am) that Jesus went out to them. I had to ask myself- why wait so long, despite seeing their struggles? Was it because He had not yet finished talking with the Father? Was it because He still needed a little more time apart? Was it because He needed to wait until the right time in the circumstances of the disciples before He could intervene, so they would appreciate and understand more who He was and gain the most from their experience? Was He watching and waiting to see if they would apply themselves to lessons previously taught?

LESSON 2: *The Lord may see you struggling in your circumstances, fighting against strong opposition, yet He may still wait to intervene. It doesn't mean He is asleep or uncaring. He knows what the greater good is. God is there, friend- be patient and persevere. He will bring the victory at the right time.*

Impetuous Peter (you gotta love him) is ready and willing to try this "walking on water" thing. While his eyes are on Jesus, it's a breeze. The minute his focus shifts from the Lord to his circumstances- the wind and the waves (an apt representation of the things that distract and eat away at our confidence in God; the unchanging pressures of life) - he starts to sink. Jesus called it **doubt**. Why? Because Peter began to focus on the circumstances rather than on Jesus. How often are we guilty of that? The good thing is that Peter immediately called out… not to his friends in the boat, but to Jesus- to save him.

LESSON 3: *When you are sinking, overwhelmed by circumstances and the impossibility of your situation, call out to Jesus first! Don't seek the rescue from man (yourself included). Seek first the face of Jesus- find God's will and tap into His enabling.*

The result was immediate rescue. Jesus saves! Notice the minute they stepped into the boat, the wind ceased and they reached their destination.

LESSON 4: *Jesus can and will calm the rising waves of fear and doubt that can threaten to overwhelm you. As the songwriter said, with Him in the vessel you can smile at the storm. I will add- with Him in the vessel, you will always reach your destination, when you have yielded all to Him.*

Jesus waited until the circumstances overwhelmed the disciples so that when He came and made the difference; they would understand Who He really is, bow and worship Him, and truly be saved. Despite the miraculous feeding of over 5,000 people before their very eyes, it was not until they saw His rule over the sea and the elements that they acknowledged, "Truly, You are the Son of God". Isn't it true, though, that for many of us we have no time for God when all is going well? It is when we are in the furnace that we draw closer to God, our Source. Thank God for the things that buffet us!

The crowd that He left behind hastened to go in search of Him, while those living where He landed spread the word and took full advantage of His presence. Imagine the power of God that was in evidence - just touching His cloak brought healing.

<u>**LESSON 5:**</u> **Spending time alone with God fills you with His power to accomplish the task set before you.**

READ JOHN 6: 25 – 40

According to Jesus, why were the people looking for Him? _____
_____

What did He mean when He said to "work… for food that endures to eternal life"? _____
_____
_____

What do you think Jesus meant when He said that the Son of Man could give them food that endures to eternal life? [vs. 27]
_____
_____
_____
_____

What do you understand vs. 29 to be saying? _____
_____
_____
_____

What did the people then ask for? _____
_____

Who is the "bread of God" and where did He come from? _____
What does vs. 37 mean to you?
_____
_____

Look at vs. 39 – 40. What does this mean for you?

_____

_____

_____

In the last chapter of this study John 6: 1 informed us that the crowd was following Jesus because they saw the signs He had performed by healing the sick. It is not by chance that in verse 5 Jesus asks, "Where shall we buy bread for these people to eat?" His subsequent provision of 'bread' to feed over five thousand people was to point them to Him, the Bread of Life! Despite all these miracles, the crowd following Him remained focused only on their physical needs… what more they could get Him to do for them. Jesus tries to lift their vision from the physical (which all decay and pass away) to the spiritual (which is eternal and so will never die)… pointing them to the Bread of Life! It wasn't Moses but God who had provided Manna (which, by the way was a 'type' or 'foreshadowing' of Christ), and that was to enable them to understand that Jesus, sent down from heaven by God the Father, is the true Manna, the Bread of Heaven, that gives Life to the world. Complete satisfaction and fulfillment comes from "feeding" on Him- from reading and listening to His Word, believing it and acting upon it in obedience.

Jesus was essentially telling them to focus on and seek after that which will transform you into the image of God's Son; on the things that build up your spirit, which will qualify you to enter God's eternal kingdom. And just how do you do that? Not by working at good deeds and striving to obey, but rather by **believing** in Jesus, the One God sent. In other words, having faith in Jesus, trusting that He is who He says He is, and accepting Him and the sacrifice He made (putting Himself in your place and paying in full the penalty for sin)- this is the "work" God requires. This is the vital point – without this 'Bread', we cannot have eternal life.

In this case, seeing was not believing because even though they had Him in their presence, they still did not believe. Yet, as Jesus pointed out, the ones who believe and come to Him do so by the will of the Father; and none of those would be lost but, on the last day, will be raised to eternal life. Many of us find this teaching (i.e. predestination) offensive. After all, if it is God who decides which of us will be saved then why blame those of us who refuse? This argument is not new.

READ ROMANS 9: 14 – 23
What do we learn here?

The fact is brothers and sisters, God has the sovereign right to do with what is His, whatever He pleases... more right than we have. "It's my hair, so I can cut it. It's my tongue, so I can pierce it. It's my body, so I can do what I want with it." We like to think **we** should have sovereign control over our lives and possessions but the Sovereign God who made us all... how dare He rule sovereignly in our lives?! Actually, it's **all God's**- He made us- so really **He can** choose for us whatever purpose He has. So we come to the argument through the ages – God's predestined purpose for us versus our free will to choose. The two seem diametrically opposed yet the bible maintains both. Let us examine this today and continue in our next chapter.

READ ROMANS 8: 29 – 30
From this, who are the ones who are predestined to be conformed to Jesus' likeness? _____
What do you think this means? _____
_____
_____
_____
_____

We often forget that God is not trapped by time and space. He is from everlasting to everlasting. In other words, He has always existed and will always exist. He sees the span of our years as all in His present... He sees your end when you leave this world (and all the days before that) from before you were born. He is all-knowing… *a jus so im stie* (that's just how He is). Therefore, how I understand it, He sees all our lives through the years and knows which of us will respond in our hearts to His Son i.e. He knows before ("foreknows"). These I believe are therefore destined to bear the image of His Son. Those whom He knows beforehand will reject His gift will still find themselves fulfilling a purpose; if even only to make the riches of His grace that much more apparent to those who accept it. But He is not the one that makes us reject Him. This means that the choice remains yours. The Father continues to lovingly extend and urge us to accept His gracious invitation, drawing us to Jesus. God, in His foreknowledge may know we will sin, but that does not mean He wills us to sin – that happens as we exercise our free will and choose to do so. We are not absolved of the decision or its consequences. Sorry, in the end we can't blame God. My friend, respond to the Father's call. Look to the Son, believe in Him and have eternal life [John 6: 40].

DID YOU KNOW?
This declaration of Jesus, "I am the bread of life", is the first of seven such emphatic "I am…" declarations found in the gospel of John, which reflect God's statement to Moses in Exodus 3: 14: "I AM WHO I AM".

As we break today, pause and think about the excuses we give to God for not accepting Jesus as Lord of our lives. When we really think about it, the truth is more often than not, it boils down to not wanting to surrender control of our lives to anyone; even the One who created us and knows us better than we know ourselves. We want to be "god" of our own existence… and the more God's way interferes with what we wish to do, the greater our resistance to yield [Genesis 3: 1 - 6]. We think our excuse is valid, but really, as the writer of Ecclesiastes says, "There is nothing new under the sun". From Adam to now, we keep exchanging the glory of the Omnipotent, Omniscient One for that which has no glory at all. We want our own way, despite the fact that history repeatedly shows us that it invariably spirals into immorality, decay, disease, war and pain.

Even those of us who are Christians can fall into the trap of thinking we know better than God; and that God just doesn't "get it". But God knows where it leads, and out of love, tries to protect us from ourselves. Only in Him is there real life!

PRAYER: -

Lord, forgive our foolish, errant ways. Lord, You know it is not easy, but by Your grace, enable me to yield my life to You and trust that You really know what is best for me; after all, You knew me before I was even born and You love me. Thanks for Your patience with us, Lord.

CHAPTER 19
THE FALLING AWAY

Let us continue our study from where we left off.

READ JOHN 6: 41 – 59

What do you notice from vs. 41 and 42? _____

_____

What do we learn in vs. 45? _____

_____

What do you think Jesus was trying to tell them in vs. 46 – 51?

_____

_____

_____

What did He mean when He encouraged the people to eat His flesh and drink His blood? _____

_____

_____

The saying that "familiarity breeds contempt" is so true. Jesus was speaking to people who knew of His childhood, His mother and His father; they were not "star-struck" by Him. Since they believed they knew His origins, *"im kuda neva kum dung fram evn"* (He could not have come down from heaven). In their eyes clearly *"im lik im ed"* (He must be delusional). Jesus did not plead His case. He reiterated that the ones who accept Him and come to Him are those who the Father draws; but did you notice verse 45? He quoted from the prophet Isaiah that "**all** will be taught by God" and continued to explain that only the ones who **listen** to the Father and **learn** from Him are the ones who come to Jesus. This means that God is speaking to and teaching the truth to *everyone*. The call goes out to **all** as the Father seeks to draw men and women to His Son. The ones **who take heed** (listen and learn, which indicate understanding and acceptance) are the ones who come.

This sheds more light on that responsibility assumed by the Father in being the One who draws individuals to Jesus as it clearly indicates the responsibility of the individual to respond. The Word of God states that He desires that **all** men be saved [1Tim. 2:4]. The debate as to whether it is all God's doing or whether man has a choice has been going on for centuries and no doubt will continue. It is my personal belief that God has the sovereign right to do with His creation what He pleases but as we have seen, He allows us the right to choose. I think we just want to have it our own way (the original sin, by the way) and then not be held responsible; let's blame God instead. In the end though, who loses- God, or us? Yet, God's love for each of us is so deep that He feels the pain of that loss. He truly "desires that none should perish" [2 Peter 3 vs. 9].

Jesus then went on to establish the veracity of what He was telling them. They hadn't seen God, but He, the only One who came from God, had. Therefore He was the best person to tell them God's viewpoint, and this is it: believing in Him and in the truth of what He is saying brings eternal life. The Manna that they were putting so much emphasis on had not guaranteed eternal life to their forefathers who had fed on it- they had all still died. Feeding on Jesus would give eternal life. Jesus was speaking of spiritual things but the people were still focused on the physical.

We do not physically eat His flesh. Rather, He gave His "flesh" (was sacrificed) as the just payment for the penalty of sin (i.e. death). When we agree and accept that it was done for us, we are appropriating that sacrifice unto ourselves, effectively "feeding on this bread of life". The Jews were repulsed; they were still interpreting it in the physical. However, "eating His flesh and drinking His blood" was not an encouragement to cannibalism. Jesus essentially meant taking unto ourselves or appropriating the sacrifice of His body and the cleansing from sin that His blood bought for us, freeing us from the sentence of death (eternal separation from God), and purchasing for us pardon and thus the gift of eternal life.

Let us close off today by looking at the rest of the Chapter.

READ JOHN 6: 60 – 71

i.   Who was verse 60 referring to? _____

ii. Is there anything that struck you about Jesus' response to the crowd?
_____
_____

iii. What do you think was meant by seeing "the Son of Man ascend to where He was before"? _____
_____
_____

iv. What else do we learn in verse 64? _____
_____

v.   What was the final result here? _____
_____
_____

Very often, when we read the Scriptures and see the word 'disciple' we automatically assume only the Twelve, but really by now Jesus had a large following of people (men and women – recall Chapter 7 of our study). Jesus pointed out to the people that He was speaking of spiritual things, not the flesh (physical things). Nevertheless, He did not "water down" His words. They had the choice to accept or reject what He said, but He was not going to make it more palatable for them (no pun intended)… 'This is the truth, take it or leave it!' In verse 62 He pointed to His return to heaven (following His death and resurrection) as the proof of what He is telling them.

I see in this a ready example of that concept of "fore-knowing". Jesus, **from the beginning, knew** who did not believe and who would betray

Him (including Judas Iscariot, one of His closest followers). Yet, He never singled them out for different treatment. He loved, taught and discipled **all** just the same. The Father continues to lovingly draw us to His Son. The question is- Are you willing to say to the Lord, like the father of the possessed son in Mark 9: 24, "I do believe, help me overcome my unbelief!"?

All of us are given the opportunity to choose to believe. Notice, Jesus even offers the choice to the Twelve, His closest disciples and friends (including Judas) - "Do you want to leave too?" And here we end today with one of Simon Peter's brilliant moments. Indeed, "to whom shall we go?" Only Jesus has the words of eternal life. Peter could say that not only did they believe, they had moved to a confirmed, certain and continuing knowledge that He was indeed the Holy One of God!

As we close this time, write your thoughts and prayers here:

CHAPTER 20

FAMILY FEUDS?

When I was growing up, there were times when I didn't want any of my friends to know my family. Sometimes I felt embarrassed by the way they would argue and quarrel. I thought surely I had the most dysfunctional family ever. As I grew older, I discovered how wrong I was. In fact, it became obvious that mine was just typical of what most families go through. Now I am proud to own them. Did you know that Jesus' family was no different? The Bible makes no attempt to hide it either.

READ JOHN 7: 1 – 9

- What are we told that Jesus had to be doing and why?

  _____

  _____

- From what His brothers said, what did they think of Him?

  _____

  _____

- What explanation did Jesus give them?

  _____

  _____

Here we see Jesus "laying low", avoiding the ones who were seeking to kill Him. I don't believe this was because He was afraid of them; it was more because He had not yet completed His ministry and His time had not yet come (as He stated in verse 6). Thus we see Him exercising wisdom and restraint in the carrying out of His mission, despite the fact that it was God who had called Him to it. Isn't there a lesson for us in this? *Resistance and rejection may face us, even though the mission we are carrying out is ordained by God; and sometimes we may have to wait, or even withdraw for a season as wisdom dictates.* This is being led by the Spirit, being submitted to Him, because the building of the Kingdom is God's work. We must be alert and always listening.

His brothers by now knew about the miracles He performed and realized that with His growing renown and consequent following, He was suitable for public office. In their eyes He was a potential ruler of the Jewish people, but certainly not Messiah; after all, they grew up with Him. Nevertheless, this was a far better estimation of Jesus on their part than they had of Him earlier on in His ministry.

READ MARK 3: 20 – 34

* What did Jesus' family think of Him [vs. 21]? _____
  _____

* What did the teachers of the law think of Him? _____
  _____

* Sum up in one sentence Jesus' response to their conclusions.
  _____
  _____

* What do you think verse 29 means?
  _____
  _____

* Which members of His family came for Him? _____
  _____

* What do you think of His response?
  _____
  _____

I can just imagine it. Mary at home with her younger children (Jesus being the first born) while neighbours and friends kept bringing news of what her eldest had been saying and doing. Can you hear one of His brothers urging her – "Ma, we have to go and get Him! He has clearly lost His mind…going around claiming to be from heaven and insinuating He is the Christ. It's embarrassing! He is bringing down the family name, making all of us look bad. If He keeps going on like this, He is going to get Himself killed. Come, let's get Him and bring Him home; get Him some help before it's too late." Can you see the real human beings behind the super-spiritual façade we have often placed on them?

This account in Mark would have been very early in Jesus' ministry, shortly after He appointed the Twelve. His brothers must have been mortified at what was happening to their older brother. Recall in Chapter 14 of our study when we looked at Mark 6: 1 – 5, where Jesus pointed out that a prophet was without honour in His hometown and among His family. Jesus saw their unbelief and understood. I don't believe He was being rude when He declared that the ones who were His mother and brothers (i.e. His family) were the ones who obeyed God [Mark 3: 34 – 35]. He was just always focused on His mission and the fact that He was about His Father's business… and it was true: it is believers who comprise God's family.

What we just read in John shows the gradual transformation that had been occurring in them. They no longer saw Him as a lunatic but rather, given His power and influence, now saw Him as a potential leader in society. His sisters were not mentioned here, but I wonder if they all felt the same way. Some may even question whether Mary had forgotten all those "words" spoken to her before and after Jesus' birth – but wouldn't that be so human?

The "unforgiveable sin" has been another talking point of strong ideas and theological discussions through the ages. Many are still in mortal fear of "using the Lord's Name in vain", despite not having a clear understanding of what that means. Indeed, how does one blaspheme against the Holy Spirit? I do not propose to tell you that I have the answer; but I will share what I believe it means.

The best explanation I have heard and the one I believe to be correct looks at the work of the Holy Spirit.

READ JOHN 16: 8; 2 THESS. 2: 13; JOHN 16: 13; & EPHESIANS 1: 13
From these passages, list some of the activities of the Holy Spirit. _____

_____

_____

What role does He play in our salvation? _____

_____

It is the Holy Spirit that convicts us of guilt with regard to sin [John 16: 8]; He is the One who sanctifies us [2 Thess. 2: 13]; He is the One who guides us into all truth [John 16: 13], explaining the deep things of God to us; and He is our seal, a deposit guaranteeing our inheritance in God's kingdom [Eph. 1: 13]. If we therefore, like those teachers of the law, attribute the work of the Spirit to Satan, it means we would reject our very means of salvation, denying that we are sinners in need of a Saviour; calling it a lie from the pit of hell. We would never then be forgiven; we would be eternally lost. Take a look at **Hebrews 10: 26 – 31**. Doesn't this corroborate this explanation? What do you think?

All that Christ was able to do was done through the Holy Spirit and despite the good that was evident, the leaders preferred to attribute such work to Satan because they were offended by Jesus. Isn't this something that we see happening today? We choose the lifestyles we want to live and if and when we find out that what we are doing goes against God's Word, we become offended. As mentioned before, we may cast all kinds of aspersions on the one who may have had the gall to point it out; we reject His Word and insist that the Bible did not originate with God but with man; or that a lot of its precepts are borrowed pagan practices, refusing to honestly seek out the truth of its historical background and the myriad proofs that exist within and without it that serve to authenticate it. I am convinced that this Word of God can stand up to any earnest and honest challenge, providing that the seeker is open to having any preconceived ideas erased. Like many before you, you will find that this Word has and IS Life.

Returning to Jesus' family – just to let you know that they did eventually believe. When we had looked at Jesus' disciples in Chapter 7, we noted that His mother Mary was included in the disciples gathered together and praying in Acts 1: 13 & 14. In addition, the book of James (thought to be the earliest of the New Testament books) was written by Jesus' brother. James was specifically named as one of the select individuals to whom Jesus appeared after the resurrection [1 Corinth. 15: 7]. He was listed as one of the apostles in the early church by Paul [Gal. 1: 19] and a member of the Council in Jerusalem [Acts 15: 13] that appeared to have overarching responsibility for the early church.

The writer of the book of Jude (another form of the Hebrew "Judah" and equivalent Greek "Judas") is also believed to be another of Jesus' brothers. He identifies himself as the brother of James; and Paul mentions Jesus' brothers among those who were leaders in the church [1 Corinth. 9: 5]. Isn't God's grace amazing? While we have breath, there is time and opportunity to turn and believe.

PRAYER: -
Father, I thank You for my family. We don't always agree, and oftentimes we treat each other worse than we do those outside our home. Yet, in family You have provided a place that holds a hope of acceptance, a refuge; a place where we are known for exactly who we are. Lord, may it be a place where I always find love and protection, and encouragement. May we all come to know You and accept Jesus' sacrifice for our salvation. Strengthen and protect my family, Lord. (Add your own prayers for your family).

CHAPTER 21
ASSUMPTIONS & ACCUSATIONS

We last saw Jesus being encouraged by His brothers to capitalize on the exposure that the Feast in Jerusalem would afford. At the time, Jesus pointed out that it was not the right time, and so they went up without Him.

READ JOHN 7: 10 – 52
Summarize the series of events.

• Any thoughts as to why Jesus may have decided to go after all?
  _____
  _____

• What does verse 13 suggest? _____
  _____
  _____

• A) What do we learn in verse 17?
  _____
  _____

  B) What do you think it means?
  _____

_____
_____
_____

- Do you believe the crowd's denial in verse 20? _____
- A) What seems to have been the main "bone of contention" that the Jews had with Jesus? [vs. 21 – 23] _____
_____

  B) What did Jesus point out in His response to it?
_____
_____
_____

- List the various responses to Jesus outlined in the passage.
_____
_____
_____
_____
_____

- What was meant in verses 37 – 39?
_____
_____
_____
_____

- What were the factors listed in the passage that caused the people to question whether Jesus could really be the Messiah? _____
_____
_____

- What is your opinion of the attitude and behaviour of the Pharisees in all this? _____
_____
_____

So here we have Jesus rejecting the advice given Him by his brothers that He should take advantage of the 'limelight' afforded Him at the Feast of Tabernacles. They therefore went on to the Feast without Him, but then He did go later, in secret. No explanation is given in the text so we are left to surmise, but I believe He was simply following His Father's instructions. Notice that before He even exposed His presence there, people were already looking expectantly for Him and discussing Him, though cautiously. It was evident that no one wanted to be considered a follower lest the Jewish authorities start taking interest in them too. Halfway through the Feast, He made His presence known and continued to show Himself an enigma. How could this carpenter know so much without having studied? Jesus pointed to God as His Source.

The importance of man's choice is again evident in verse 17. It is the one who **chooses** to obey God who will, as a result of that choice, understand the truth and know that Jesus is sent by God. Jesus pointed out that He had no hidden agenda. Unlike political leaders who are seeking a following, He was not seeking anything for Himself; rather, He was seeking glory for God. Yet they were trying to kill Him.

I am personally not convinced that they didn't know of the intention to kill Him. From verse 13, they certainly knew He was persona non grata, since they were all so afraid to speak publicly about Him for fear of reprisals. This meant they must have known that the Jewish leaders were after Him (as was confirmed later in the chapter). Verse 25 even highlighted the confusion of those who couldn't understand how He was being allowed to speak so publicly. I think, in their effort to distance themselves from the truth of what He was saying, they lashed out at Him, calling Him demon-possessed. Malign Him and His character so that no one would take His words seriously, even if they happened to be true.

Typical of Jesus, He didn't back down or try to defend Himself. He stated the exact reason that had brought them to that position and showed the error of their reasoning: How could you want to kill Him for desecrating the Sabbath when all He had done was show mercy on that day? As was the case with circumcision, there were some things that superceded the observance of the Day; judge rightly!

We also see the varying points of view. Some felt He was a good man; others labelled Him a deceiver [vs. 12]. The sight of Him speaking so boldly in public, without anyone restraining Him, led some to wonder if the authorities had concluded that He was indeed the Christ. This strongly suggests that there were many who were taking their cue from the Jewish leaders. However, don't miss their 'stumbling blocks': "but we know where He came from" and the Christ was not supposed to come from Galilee but from Bethlehem. They were coming to the wrong conclusions because they were basing them on incorrect **assumptions** and not necessarily on facts.

For the Pharisees, it appears their pride was their downfall. They were the ones learned in the Law and therefore felt they knew what was best… and they would entertain no opposition. How dare the temple guards think they know better than these learned men! Even Nicodemus, one of their own, was a target for their anger. Rather than listen to his voice of reason, they chose to attack him personally, exposing their prejudice.

As you may have realized, the reference to 'The Prophet' we discussed already in Chapter 17.

BRINGING IT HOME: -
Have you ever felt attacked by any person or persons because of assumptions they have made about you, your upbringing, your beliefs, or motives? Have they maligned your character without bothering to find out the truth?
Have you been guilty of doing that to anyone, without even realizing it?

One area where the Lord showed me I was guilty of this was in regards to some of my relationships. If, for example, I expected someone to do something and they didn't, before finding out the reason they were unable to, I would assume a logical reason. Then in my head I would build up a list of associated incursions and a winning argument, usually condemning the individual before they had even been given a chance to explain. This was especially true when there were trust issues either with that individual or from past experiences with other individuals in the same situation.

Let me give a hypothetical example from let's say a personal relationship, as this is a common occurrence. Mary, having been in a previous relationship with someone who proved unfaithful, is now in a new relationship with Joe. They agree to meet for dinner at 5 p.m. Mary arrives on time and sits waiting. More than half an hour passes and she begins to worry. She tries to call Joe and initially the phone rings and rings before going to voicemail. As more time passes, she tries again but now the phone does not even ring and it is clear to her that he has turned off the instrument. Her thoughts start to recollect how it had been with her previous boyfriend. What was initially concern turns to anger as she asks herself if he didn't have the decency to call and say he would be late. She starts to wonder if he is with someone else and then feels certain that that is the reason he turned off the phone. She sorts through in her mind the many ways he could have contacted her and begins to plan all her retorts for whatever excuses he comes with. By the time Joe arrives one hour late, the air is frozen with ice. He opens his mouth to apologize but he barely gets the words out before she 'tears' into him for his lack of consideration, just stopping short of accusing him of being with some girl. Joe begins to get defensive and turned off… 'Who is this person?' To shorten the story, it turns out he was called to a late meeting and left his phone on his desk, not expecting the meeting to last that long. His co-worker hears the phone ringing but, respecting his privacy, chooses not to answer it and eventually turns it off so that it would not disturb him anymore. Joe rushes from his meeting, knows he is late, so he grabs his phone and personal belongings and rushes to his dinner date…only to face 'blazing Mary'. Though fiction, it would be funny, if it weren't so true and so common; maybe different scenarios but all along a similar line… and both sexes are guilty of it. This is a common cause of rifts in marriages, in workplaces; even in churches… offense is taken over what turns out to be mere assumptions. We fall headfirst into the plan of the enemy. Do I hear an "OUCH"?

Jesus was faced with assumptions made about Him from both within His family and from outsiders. He however did not let those assumptions dictate His actions, no matter that they led to accusations of Him being mad or demon-possessed. We see today that this can really hurt an individual. Let us be careful not to base our actions on things we assume. In the end we are the ones who look foolish.

Memory verse: John 7: 24
"Stop judging by mere appearances, and make a right judgment."

PRAYER: -

(Is there anything you wish to confess to the Lord today? Or maybe you want to ask Him to reveal to you where you may have been guilty of accusing someone wrongfully? Have you lost precious friendships because of this? I found that He was quite able to break me out of the habit of coming to the wrong conclusions and helping me to give others the benefit of the doubt. It makes for a much less stressful existence.)

CHAPTER 22

"I AM"

Wow! Look how far we've come. We've seen Jesus turn water into wine (and of the best quality at that); we've seen Him speak the Word of healing from a distance to the official's son [John 4], as well as bring restoration to an invalid after 38 years [John 5]. He fed over 5,000 people from a small morsel and demonstrated His power over nature by walking on water. His teachings have left His hearers astounded at its wisdom; and we have seen Him declare that anyone who thirsts should come to Him and drink, becoming channels of living water. Indeed, those who partake would never thirst again, having been filled with the Holy Spirit. Despite mounting opposition and threats to Himself, He continued to teach.

READ JOHN 7: 53 – 8: 11
- Who brought the woman? _____
- What was her crime? _____
- Do you notice anything missing from this scenario? _____
- Do you understand what trap they were setting for Jesus?

_____

_____

_____

_____

- What, if anything, impresses you about His response?

_____

_____

The NIV points out that this particular passage very likely does not belong in the flow of the gospel of John at this point. It does not mean the incident never happened; it just originally may have been a part of another narrative. It certainly remains true to what we have seen of Jesus thus far.

The Pharisees dragged this woman into the middle of the Temple court and forced her to stand in front of everyone [vs. 3], clearly determined to humiliate her as well as stir up the crowd. Given the sin she was being accused of – adultery, her "partner in crime" was noticeably absent! How do you catch one person in the act of adultery? Obviously, they had allowed the man to escape giving credence to the notion that this was all a set-up to trap Jesus. How, you may ask? Well, they believed Jesus would have one of two options in responding. Either He would agree that she deserved death by stoning as the Jewish Law prescribed, or conversely, reject it, confirming Himself a law-breaker. If He chose the former, He would have given way to the principle of the dominance of the *letter* of the law, thus showing Himself no different from the Pharisees and teachers of the law. All His teachings on mercy and forgiveness would then mean nothing and His ministry would be undermined. They wanted to diffuse the effectiveness of His ministry. Added to this, only the Roman rulers could carry out the death penalty. If Jesus had instructed them to stone her, He would have gotten in trouble with Rome. If He had absolved her, they would have proven to the crowd that He had no respect for Jewish law. Either way, they could be rid of Him.

What a picture of contrasts: the teachers of the law, zealous and full of righteous indignation; Jesus, calm and contemplative. The former uncaring about the life of this woman and determined to humiliate her; the latter lovingly extending mercy- condemning the sin but not the sinner. Jesus turned it into a test for the Pharisees themselves. The older and wiser heads knew they were all sinful too and led the way for the younger folk. Because of Jesus, this woman experienced mercy and another chance at life. He didn't consider her worthless and so easily discarded. No wonder He was followed by a retinue of women. He restored their person-hood and demonstrated God's view of the female gender. He didn't condone her sin [vs. 11] but He didn't condemn her.

READ JOHN 8: 12 – 30

- What does Jesus declare Himself to be? _____
- In your own words, what does that mean?

  _____

  _____

  _____

- Who are the witnesses confirming that what Jesus is saying is true?

  _____

- What is Jesus pointing out in verse 19? _____

  _____

- Who is Jesus claiming to be in verses 24 & 28? _____
- What is the consequence for the one who rejects that claim?

  _____

- What do we learn about the relationship between Jesus and His Father in this passage? _____

  _____

  _____

The light of the world- dispelling the darkness, exposing what is hidden, stirring up and bringing forth new life this is the second 'I am' statement that Jesus made, as recorded in John's gospel. He rejected the Pharisees judgment because it was based on external appearances, without knowing all the facts. Jesus, though not judging them at the time, was in a better position to do so because God the Father was with Him and it would be the testimony of the two of them As such, their judgment fulfilled the criteria in the Law that a matter be established on the testimony of two or three witnesses [Deuteronomy 19: 15]. Can you appeal to anyone higher than God?

Jesus drives home the connection between Himself and the Father: to know Him is to know the Father. Recall at the start of our study when it was established that "In the beginning… the Word was with God and the Word was God". Jesus was declaring and claiming to be just that- the Messiah, "God with Us", and verse 24 leaves us with no "out". If you do not believe in Him, you will die in your sins, unforgiven; facing eternal death and separation from God.

"Free Indeed"

READ JOHN 8: 31 – 47

- What does verse 31 indicate?

  _____

  _____

  _____

- Are you presently a slave to anything or anyone? (Stop and think about it.)
  - o Your job
  - o Material things
  - o Your partner/spouse
  - o Bad Habit/s
  - o Persistent sin
  - o Your past
  - o Tradition
  - o Fears
  - o Becoming rich
  - o What others think of you
  - o Other
- Who are the two fathers mentioned in verses 38 & 41?

  _____

- What information about the devil do we get here?

  _____

  _____

  _____

- What do you think about verse 47?

  _____

  _____

Lip service is no guarantee. Saying you believe does not make you a Christian. "Holding to" i.e. obeying Him- that is what counts; and those who do are the ones who understand the truth that sets them free from sin and the baggage that comes with it. Jesus came to set us free: from sin and separation from God; from guilt and bondage; and from chasing after that which can never satisfy.

As Jesus tried to point out to them the state of their hearts, they appeared to lash out. Some believe the statement "We are not illegitimate children" to be a barb at Jesus' earthly beginnings. If it was, do you notice that Jesus seemed to ignore it? His assertion that they were unable to hear (understand) what He was saying reminds me of **1 Corinthians 2: 14:** *"The man without the Spirit does not accept the things that come from the Spirit of God, for they are foolishness to him, and he cannot understand them, because they are spiritually discerned" (memorize).* Thus, indeed, the one "who belongs to God hears what God says".

READ JOHN 8: 48 – 59
Why is it that when the truth hits a nerve, we lash out at the speaker? Jesus bore the brunt of their anger.

What does verse 51 mean?

_____

_____

_____

_____

Jesus, because He cannot lie, would not dilute His message to please His hearers. Here we come to His third "I am" statement which leaves no doubt in the minds of His listeners what He is really saying.

Paraphrase verse 58:

_____

_____

_____

_____

Jesus made it clear: before Abraham ever even existed… **I AM!** Not I was. No, the present continuous I AM. In other words, as God declared to Moses in Exodus 3: 14 His Name ("I AM has sent you"), so Jesus repeats it: I have always existed and will always be…I AM! He was unequivocally stating that He is God! That is why they wanted to stone Him, because they had now convicted Him of blasphemy.

BRINGING IT HOME: -

Jesus came to set the captives free. All of us were captive to sin and many of us are still experiencing the consequences, despite receiving Christ as Lord and Saviour. Some of us don't even realize we are in bondage, so accustomed are we to our chains. Prayerfully ask God to reveal to you any areas of bondage that remain, and to lead you into the freedom He has already won for you. Remember His perspective of the woman caught in the act of adultery... His mercy is boundless.

Pause here now and consider how your view of Jesus has been expanding. Do you see Him any differently? If so, what has changed? Does it give you a clearer appreciation of His work in your life?

You may write your thoughts here:

PRAYER: -

Lord, I thank You that Your compassion, care and concern are constant and consistent. Lord, You do not treat us the way we deserve, given our sin and repeated rebellion. Your heart's desire is indeed for us to be free. God, I expose and turn over my life to You. Wash and purify me, remove all guilt and self-condemnation. Let me walk as I truly am- FREE! Help me to remember that You are not bound by time and space; that You have known all my days from before I was even born, yet You loved me and came after me. I am so in awe of such love. Thank You, Jesus. I love You.

CHAPTER 23

BLINDNESS

READ JOHN 9: 1 – 34

- Based on verse 2, what was the prevailing belief at the time?

  _____

  _____

  _____

- Can you think of any misconceptions that presently exist about evil, God, and the way He works?

  _____

  _____

  _____

  _____

- What do you think Jesus meant by what He said in verse 4?

  _____

  _____

- Why was the man taken before the Pharisees? _____

  _____

- From verse 16, what conflict did the Pharisees have?

  _____

  _____

- Despite the man's own testimony about himself, the Jews refused to believe a healing had occurred. Why do you think this was so?

  _____

  _____

- What impression have you made of :
  i.   The man's parents? _____
      _____
  ii. The man himself? _____
      _____
      _____

- Comment on verses 28 – 34.
  _____
  _____

Here we see a vivid demonstration of Jesus being the light of the world, illuminating the darkness of this precious child of God who we are told was born blind. Note the prevailing thought of the day was that either the sins of this man or of his parents must be the cause of his disability. Jesus threw aside the myth and explained that it was an opportunity to demonstrate God's power. Very often we wonder at some of the situations that occur in people's lives, sometimes even in our own lives; and we question God's character and His love, or even His existence. However, God sees the bigger picture and when we see Him resolve the situation, we come face to face with the reality of the sovereignty and awesomeness of this great God. Therefore Jesus encouraged His disciples (and us) to take every opportunity while we are here on earth to display the work of God in and to those around us.

I find the cast of characters in this account so interesting. We see his neighbours and onlookers stunned and surprised, even disbelieving that this man can now see; so impossible it seemed. Yet they brought him before the Pharisees because the incident occurred on the Sabbath. The ritualistic following of the letter of the law again took precedence over any empathy or rejoicing at his good fortune. Now, here we see the dilemma the Pharisees faced. If this man (Jesus) is evil (which they concluded He must be since He was breaking the Sabbath), how come He is doing so much good? So unmoving were some of them in their assessment of Him that they would rather believe that no miracle had occurred and this man was never born blind [vs. 18]. They didn't want to face the only conclusion they were left with if indeed this man had been miraculously healed... but he was, and they couldn't change that fact. His parents confirmed it and the man himself insisted it was so. The parents, however, did not want to be brought into the *"kas kas"* (quarrel).

Above all, I love the innocent truth from the man himself. As a good friend once said to me, "The man with an experience is never at the mercy of a man with an argument". The Pharisees could not sway him; he knew what he had experienced! He was not prepared to cast any judgment on the One who healed him [vs. 25], all he knew was that once he was blind but now he could see! Because he would not bend to their assertions, the Pharisees cursed him too [vs. 28]; and when they could not find any reasonable argument to his conclusion [vs. 30 – 33], they proceeded to attack his character. They had no other response to the obvious:-

Jesus had healed him, of that he was sure; and healing could only come from God. Therefore, this man must be from God! How remarkable that these teachers of the Law couldn't see it?! [vs. 30]

Worse, to have it pointed out by this unlearned 'peasant' was more than their pride could stand [vs. 34]!

> **BRAATA:-**
> Are there any lessons you can learn from this man who had been healed?
> Stop and think about it.

READ JOHN 9: 35 – 41
Write your thoughts.

It struck me that because this man had experienced a demonstration of God's power; his heart was more open to hearing and receiving Jesus. He moved from thinking of Jesus as just a man, to a prophet, then to being the Son of God, Messiah. His final response was to worship Him. Jesus, having healed him of his physical blindness, then healed him of his spiritual blindness… but he was willing to see. Not so the Pharisees, who could not see that they were indeed blind, despite having the truth shown to them. They were therefore without excuse- how much greater their judgment?!

READ JOHN 10: 1 – 21

- Which two "I Am" statements do you identify here?
  - i. _____
  - ii. _____
- List the features of the shepherd:

  _____
  _____
  _____
  _____
  _____
  _____
  _____

- Who are the other sheep referred to in vs. 16? _____

Here we find two more "I Am" statements. Jesus is both 'the gate' to the sheep pen and 'the good shepherd'. The sheep pen (which I believe represents the kingdom of God) is a safe and protected environment in which the sheep are held. We are the sheep; at least, those of us who belong to Him are. Anyone who comes to guide the sheep but does not enter through the gate is a thief and a robber. Thus, anyone who doesn't come in the Name of Jesus or through Him, the gate- can immediately be recognized as an imposter.

Note especially verse 9- only those who enter through the gate (Jesus Christ) will be saved. In other words, you can only enter the kingdom through Jesus Christ. He knows those who are His; He can call them by name and they know His voice. This indicates relationship. I am struck by the fact that He does not drive His sheep, beating and cajoling them, nor dragging them kicking and screaming. There is no element of force.

Rather, He simply leads and they follow [vs. 4]. In addition, because they walk in relationship with Him, they can distinguish His voice from that of a stranger and therefore will not be led astray.

> **BRAATA:** *This was in fact the way shepherds treated their sheep. They would spend time with and sleep among the flock, deliberately getting to know each sheep personally. As a result the sheep became familiar with the shepherd and could identify his voice. Eventually the shepherd could stand outside the sheep pen and call each sheep by name. Only his sheep would respond. Relationship has to be deliberately and painstakingly developed!*

Any who had come before Jesus and claimed to be Messiah were deceivers. Jesus' coming provided not just life, but life in abundance!

We need to remember that this treatise followed on from His conversation with the Pharisees in chapter 9: 39- 41. These men, being learned in the Law and Prophets, should have understood clearly what He was alluding to in Chapter 10.

READ EZEKIEL 34: 1 – 24

* Who do you think were the shepherds of Israel [vs.2]?

  _____

* What were they guilty of?

  _____

* What had been expected of them?

  _____

* What therefore was the judgment on the shepherds?

  _____

* What would the Lord Himself do for His sheep?

  _____

  _____

  _____

* Who was verse 23 pointing to? _____

Those in positions of leadership should take note of this passage. The kings, priests and prophets who had been left in charge of God's people, Israel, had feathered their own nests, getting 'fat' while the people (the flock) suffered and strayed, and were eventually exiled. Note that both the shepherds and the sheep were judged; in fact, even those who did not follow God (rams and goats- which I interpret to mean the Gentile nations and their rulers)did not escape His judgment. God is a God of justice and is concerned about all. I believe this passage makes it clear that leaders will be held accountable.

This prophetic word was given to Ezekiel while Judah was exiled in Babylon. It promised Israel that God would gather them back from all the places they had been scattered, and He would place over them one Shepherd, David. Now David had lived and died centuries before; so this could not have been speaking of King David, himself. However, recall what we discussed in the second chapter of our study. This prophecy was in fact speaking to one of David's future descendants, who would be king and ruler i.e. Messiah.

Let us return then to John 10. When Jesus declared "I am the good shepherd"; not the hired hand (like the present leaders of Israel i.e. the Pharisees, etc.), but the owner of the sheep, He was telling them that He was in fact the Messiah. More than that, He would willingly die for His sheep; and not just the sheep from this sheep pen (the Jews), but also other sheep from another sheep pen [vs.16] i.e. us, Gentiles. God had sent Him to do that and He would do it willingly of His own accord; nobody would be taking His life from Him.

Now, look at a very familiar passage:

READ PSALM 23
Looking at the activity of the shepherd in this psalm, do you see the work of the "good shepherd" in your life at present?

If so, how?

Are you familiar with His voice?

READ JOHN 10: 22 – 42

Just imagine!! They ask Him to state plainly if He is Messiah; yet when He does confirm it, they attempt to stone Him for blasphemy ("I and the Father are one."). Clearly they didn't believe Him. At the same time, they could not deny the miracles He had performed, but they were "tripping" over the word God. The passage Jesus quotes comes from Psalm 82 where in verse 6, the rulers of Israel are called "gods, sons of the Most High", indicating that they were placed in their positions of authority by God. Jesus' argument is that if they could be called that, how much moreso Him. Surely the miracles prove that He is working on behalf of God.

Another thing I feel compelled to point out is that though He was speaking to Jews, He said they were not His sheep and that is the reason they didn't believe Him. This means that not all Israel were His sheep, but only those who followed Him. The imperative of knowing and hearing His voice is critical in this regard. Let those of us in the church take note!

Jesus left this 'seat of knowledge' and returned to being among the common folk. They, not being puffed up with pride from thinking they knew it all, were open to listening, and so believed.

PRAYER: -

Father, may I never be so full of myself, that I become unteachable. Keep me from thinking I know so much that I limit Your ability to show me new and different things. Remind me that true wisdom and knowledge come from You. Open my eyes to see Your work and actions in my life and open my ears to hear You speak. Thank You for shedding light into my darkness.

CHAPTER 24

"I AM THE RESURRECTION & THE LIFE"

I hope I haven't lost you. Sometimes, we start off with great gusto and excitement as we embark upon a new study or project, but somewhere in the middle we start to get tired or distracted. I pray that you will press in and press on. Don't let the devil snatch away this opportunity to draw closer to Jesus. I am confident you will gain much and build up your spirit as we continue. May the Holy Spirit breathe new life into your time spent with Him in the Word.

READ JOHN 11: 1 – 44

- From the opening verses, what can you infer about the relationship between Jesus and this family? _____ _____

  _____

- What was the disciples' chief concern? _____
- What do you think Jesus meant in verses 9 & 10?

  _____

  _____

  _____

- Why did Jesus wait before going to Martha and Mary? _____
- Picture the scenes described in verses 17 – 44. What are the things that stand out in your mind? _____

  _____

  _____

  _____

_____

_____

_____

Jesus obviously had a very close relationship with this family. Notice the message that was sent to Jesus to inform Him that the one He loved was sick [vs.3]. Luke 10: 38 – 42 records a previous visit of Jesus to their home, where Martha did her best to ensure that the needs of He and His disciples were met. His interaction with the sisters in this passage in John's gospel reflects a close relationship. Yet, Jesus waited, despite knowing what they would have to go through.

What about you? Do you feel like you have been waiting a very long time; past hope, even despair? Do your thoughts repeatedly question God? - Why? How long, Lord? Are you saying 'No'? Blessed one, don't lose faith in this God you have come to believe in. ALL His actions proceed out of love, for that is who He is. It may make no sense whatsoever to us, but rest in the knowledge that He sees the bigger picture. Even when it doesn't go the way you planned or hoped – trust His heart!

Since they had tried to stone Him when He last ministered in Jerusalem, the disciples were fearful of Him being killed should He venture near there again. Jesus, however, moved only to the beat of God's drum. He would not be rushed to respond to the urgent plea of Mary and Martha, nor be discouraged by the fear of His disciples. His remarks in verses 9 & 10 seem to reflect what He had said previously in John 9: 4 – 5, when He declared that He was the light of the world. There seems to be a dual meaning to His statement in that as long as the sun (the light of the world) shone providing daylight, one would not stumble because one can see; in the same way, while He (the Light of the world) was alive and present with them, He was their guide so they could not fall. The ones who rejected Him, who did not have the 'Light' (and therefore walked in darkness) would stumble.

Jesus' timing allowed for Lazarus to be dead long enough for decay to set in. No one could therefore offer any other reasonable explanation for the rising of this obviously dead man, than that Jesus could restore life-something that only God could do. So we come to the sixth emphatic "I Am" statement in the book of John: "I Am resurrection and life" (the original Greek has no definite article). This was an important point to drive home because it would further cement the faith and belief in Jesus of those who followed Him. It was a confirmation that He must be Messiah, sent from God, because only God gives life.

Jesus' words in verse 4 were particularly poignant because, though they spoke to Lazarus' resurrection bringing glory to God and to Jesus; they seemed to also reflect on Jesus' own upcoming death and resurrection. This would unquestionably declare His power and bring glory to Himself and through Him, to God. In fact, this last 'sign' (as John's gospel describes the miracles He performed) marked the turning point in Jesus' ministry; the "final nail in His coffin", so to speak.

READ JOHN 11: 45 – 57
- What two responses to Lazarus' resurrection are mentioned here?

  _____

  _____

- What was the primary concern of the Sanhedrin?

  _____

  _____

- What do you think of Caiaphas' declaration in verse 50?

  _____

  _____

- What did he unwittingly prophesy? _____

- What was the final conclusion of the meeting? _____

  _____

The raising of Lazarus, according to the gospel of John, marked the turning point in the ministry of Jesus. The Jewish leaders were now determined that He must die; otherwise the Romans would see Him as a threat to their sovereignty and as one who was stirring up rebellion against Caesar. They would come against the entire Jewish nation and its leaders to squash any such rebellion. These Jewish leaders would therefore lose their place of prominence. Caiaphas, then, was speaking to this in his declaration in verse 50. However, he unknowingly was also prophesying Jesus' death to take away the sins of His people Israel, indeed of all those from every nation who would believe and accept His sacrifice [verses 51 & 52]. Aren't you astounded that the awesome miracle of Lazarus' resurrection seemed to have been completely lost on these leaders? Let me point out, by the way, that Caiaphas was a Sadducee, and Sadducees did not believe in the resurrection [c.f. Matt. 22: 23]. The raising of Lazarus must have seriously undermined his credibility in the eyes of the people. I wonder if this contributed to his judgment that Jesus must die.

From this point on, we see a steady movement of Jesus to the cross.

BRINGING IT HOME:
Is there anything in your life that needs resurrecting: a long-held desire that you have now shelved; a calling on your life that has been so long in finding fulfillment that you have discarded it and moved on; a marriage; your Christian walk? Do you believe that Jesus really is the resurrection and the life? What does He have to say about it? Why not at least find out?

One final note before we move on. It struck me that after Jesus called forth Lazarus He instructed others, not Lazarus, to remove the grave clothes. Given how bodies were prepared for burial, it would have been difficult for Lazarus to walk, much less remove his wrappings. Sometimes after we have been given new life in Christ, it is the body of Christ- the church i.e. the community of believers who must help to 'loose us and let us go'. This, I believe is an important part of the function of the church [Acts 26:18].

John's gospel then tells us of Jesus being anointed by Mary (Lazarus' sister) at Bethany. We already looked at this when we compared and contrasted it with a similar event done by 'a sinful woman' in Chapter 15 of our study: "Are You the One?" Suffice it to say here that Jesus declared it a preparation for His burial, pointing to His upcoming death. More and more, we will see Jesus speaking openly about this as He prepares His disciples for His departure.

READ LUKE 18: 31 – 34

i.   What does Jesus prophesy? _____

_____

ii. What was the disciples' response? _____

_____

I don't think Jesus could have stated anything more clearly and succinctly. Yet it seems the disciples didn't get it. Were they in denial? It just didn't make sense in the scheme of their expectations, so they couldn't understand it. Matthew's gospel gives us more information.

READ MATTHEW 20: 17 – 28

•   What did the mother of Zebedee's sons request of Jesus?

_____

Mark's gospel has James and John (the sons of Zebedee) making the request themselves.

•   What do you think they were really asking for? _____

_____

•   Why were the other disciples upset with the brothers? _____

_____

_____

•   What lesson on leadership did Jesus use the opportunity to teach?

_____

_____

Jesus, like a good leader, starts to prepare His disciples for what is about to happen. So detailed is His prophecy that He is able to tell them that it is not the Jews stoning Him that will kill Him; rather, they will hand Him over to the Gentiles (the Romans) and He would be mocked, spat upon, flogged and crucified... but He would rise again three days later.

Looking at the two passages together, either the disciples didn't believe He would die or could not bear the thought of Him dying, because it didn't fit into their concept of who Messiah was... or they chose to focus on Him being raised. At any rate, from the request made of Him by Zebedee's family, it is clear that they believed He was shortly about to declare His kingdom and take up the throne of Israel... and they wanted first dibs. They were still thinking in the natural. They believed that Jesus was telling them that they were heading to Jerusalem to wrest the kingdom of Israel out of the clutches of Rome and seize rulership over Jerusalem. Their request was to make them His "right-hand men", co-regents, second (and third?) in command. That is why the other disciples were indignant- how dare they?! (No doubt, they harbored aspirations of holding those posts themselves.)

The ensuing dialogue about drinking from the same cup had Jesus speaking of spiritual things while James and John were thinking in the physical realm. Little did they know how much indeed they would have to go through. The disciples began to argue but Jesus calmed them by putting God's perspective on it. Godly leaders don't put themselves above those they lead. Rather the one who wants to lead is to be servant, just as Jesus Himself was.

So Jesus and His disciples started to head for Jerusalem and to the cross. At Jericho a blind man (Bartimaeus) received his sight when he persisted in calling out to Jesus for mercy, despite being rebuked by the crowd [Mark 10: 46 – 52; Luke 18: 35 – 43]. There too a tax collector named Zacchaeus repented of his sin and received salvation. Jesus then took the opportunity to teach.

READ LUKE 19: 11 – 27
- Who do you think the man of noble birth represented? _____
- What instructions were given to his servants? _____

_____

_____

_____

- Who hated him? _____

- What do you notice about the rewards given to the servants?
  _____

- What excuse did the third servant give? _____
  _____

- What was the master's response? _____
  _____

- Who do you think the servants represent in the parable?
  _____
  _____

- Who are the subjects? _____
- Summarize then what you think Jesus was saying to the crowd when
  He spoke this parable: _____
  _____
  _____
  _____
  _____

Jesus never explained this parable and I wonder if the crowd understood its implications. Verse 11 gives us the first clue by setting the background for the telling of this story. Note, He was near Jerusalem and the people who were following Him thought He was going to declare His Kingship and take up rule, defeating Rome. Jesus, however, in this veiled way was letting them know that yes, He would be king, but not now. He would be going away first. Note also the difference between His servants and His subjects.

The ones who followed Him, believed in Him and served Him were each given a mina i.e. all got equivalent capital to invest and multiply. The one who gained the greatest interest would be put in charge of more when the master returned as king. The one who 'sat on' the investment, not utilizing it and gaining nothing would be judged for doing so, and would lose everything. It seemed to me that there was no acceptable excuse for doing so – fear was not a valid excuse. I don't believe Jesus was agreeing with the servant's estimation of His character. In fact, His response took the form of a question, essentially saying, "So **you think** I am a hard and unreasonable man, do you? Then, all the more reason to ensure that you do not cross me. You should even have put the money on a safe deposit to earn interest!"

What are the lessons for us? We who are Christians, who are believers, are His servants. All of us have been given an investment that Jesus expects to receive returns on when He comes in glory. Being afraid is not going to be considered a valid excuse! Are you faithfully using the gifts and talents He has given, even if it is *"wan dege, dege wan"* (only one), to build His Kingdom? There will come a time of reckoning. Verse 26 makes it clear that you are accountable for what you have (including what you know to be true). Has what you have learnt in the Word made a difference in the way you live your life? Has it borne fruit? Be careful you don't lose it.

His subjects, I believe, were the Jews. It could also mean the world that He will return to judge. Either way, the ones who rejected Him as king would be killed. This reflects Revelation 20: 11 – 15, 'the second death'. I believe Jesus was already warning them. As He approaches the cross, we will see more teaching on this.

PRAYER: -
Lord, have I been disobedient? Is there anything that You have been calling me to do that I have been running away from? Show me, Lord; and help me to submit to Your will. Please, don't give up on me, Lord. Keep me from fear, and let Yourself be glorified in me.

CHAPTER 25

HOSANNA

Do you feel the 'shift in the wind'? By now word is spreading like wildfire. Can you hear the talk on the streets of Jerusalem; along the highways out in the countryside; in the temple courts; quiet whisperings in the homes – "Surely Jesus is the One. Imagine Messiah has come in our lifetime. Surely He can gather together an army to take on Caesar – we are ready! It is time! Self- rule, we can be free. God is with us. We can defeat Rome". The people saw their deliverer. Jesus saw the cross and the scourging that would precede it. Yet He moved steadily on to Jerusalem.

READ LUKE 19: 28 44 & compare to MATTHEW 21: 1 – 11 & JOHN 12: 12 – 19
From these accounts: -

i.   When did the triumphal entry occur? _____
ii. Close your eyes and try to picture the scene. Can you sense the excitement, celebration and anticipation of the crowd? Write your thoughts here. _____
   _____
   _____
   _____

iii. Why do you think Jesus chose on this occasion to enter Jerusalem riding on the back of a donkey? _____
   _____
   _____

READ ZECHARIAH 9: 9 & 10

i.   Whose king? _____

ii. What was the king proclaiming and to whom? __ _____

iii. What did his rule cover? _____

Now, return to the passages in the gospels.

i.   What did the shouts of the crowd indicate? _____

_____

ii. What do you understand from Jesus' 'lament' in Luke 19: 41 – 44?

_____

_____

John lets us know that the triumphal entry into Jerusalem occurred the day after Jesus was anointed by Mary of Bethany; and that had occurred six days before the Passover. This means He entered Jerusalem on the donkey's colt the Sunday before He would be crucified. Therefore in the next few chapters we will be looking at the last week before He died.

Though the disciples did not know it at the time, prophecy was being fulfilled – Israel's king would come to her on a young donkey, not a warhorse. For me, it signifies the prophet had foretold that He would come in peace, bringing peace; not to declare war on Israel's overlords as they anticipated. In fact, Zechariah also predicted that He would come to proclaim peace to **all** the nations, not just Israel. He would come as ruler of the whole earth.

Nevertheless, the excited crowd shouted their praise acknowledging Him as Messiah, Son of David, and the king who had come in the name of the Lord; all in anticipation of Him seizing rulership over Jerusalem. Jesus, being indeed Messiah, did not deter them since what they said was true; but His lament for Jerusalem demonstrated that He knew they had missed the point. He went on to prophesy Jerusalem's destruction which was fulfilled in AD 70, exactly as He foretold. Meanwhile, the poor Pharisees were beside themselves, seeing the adoration and large following of the crowds [John 12: 19].

Monday

The next 'stop' in the sequence of events leading up to His crucifixion was the 'second' cleansing of the temple [Mark 11: 12 – 19]. We already looked at this in Chapter 8 of our study, so now we look as Jesus boldly took on the leaders of the Jewish people.

Tuesday

READ MATTHEW 21: 23 – 32

i.   Why do you think Jesus asked them about John's ministry in response to their questioning His authority? _____

_____

_____

ii. From the parable of the 2 sons, who do you think they represented?

_____

_____

_____

We know this happened on Tuesday as Matthew 21: 18 and Mark 11: 20 tell us this happened the morning after He cleansed the temple. Given the response to Jesus of the crowds pouring into Jerusalem for the Passover feast, the chief priests and elders were understandably concerned. They didn't believe He was Messiah but obviously the people did. They therefore sought ways to trap Him. They wanted to know on whose authority He acted. Since it was on the same authority that John had ministered (i.e. God's), Jesus asked them about that. If they had answered "God's", they would also need to explain why it was that they had not followed John. They refused to answer, so Jesus went on to point out their rebellion. They were represented by the supposedly willing son, giving lip service to God, professing obedience but not actually carrying out the Father's will.

In contrast, the 'sinners' (and Jesus chose the most obvious – tax collectors and prostitutes), were the ones who were actually being obedient to God. Do you see the contrast: the 'church' leaders (chief priests and elders – the ones who by all appearances were destined for heaven) versus the ones whose lifestyles clearly rejected God's will? The former appeared to say yes to God but in actuality, the opposite was true. The leaders' hearts refused to yield while the 'sinners' were repenting.

READ MATTHEW 21: 33 – 46
- Who is the landowner? _____
- What is the vineyard? _____
- Who are the tenants? _____
- Who are the servants? _____
- Who is the son? _____
- Who are the other tenants referred to in verse 41? _____

God (the landowner), in His desire to let people know about Him and be drawn to Him, set apart the Jews, developing a relationship with them. He deposited in them His law and precepts; giving them an understanding of what His will is, to demonstrate to the world what His kingdom was all about (the vineyard). The Jews, and in particular the chief priests and elders of the people, were the caretakers (the tenants) of His vineyard. When they kept rebelling against Him, He sent the Old Testament prophets (the servants) repeatedly, but they had them killed. Finally, God sent His Son Jesus, but they killed Him too (or would soon do so, after all they were already planning to).

Thus, since the Jews were rejecting His rule, the kingdom would be placed in the hands of those who would become believers- Jews and Gentiles (other tenants) - who would bring in the harvest God desired. The stone (Jesus) the builders rejected would still become the cornerstone. This quote in verse 42 comes from Psalm 118: 22 – 23 and some commentators believe it referred to King David originally or to Israel, but Jesus here applied it to Himself. Isaiah 28: 16 gives us an understanding of what a cornerstone was used for- it made for a sure foundation. Builders would therefore assess the size and quality of a stone before choosing it for such an important role. Though the builders (the Jews) rejected Him because He did not have the appearance they were looking for (i.e. He didn't come the way they expected); yet He became the foundation on which God's

OPERATION RESCUE: MISSION ACCOMPLISHED

church (His Kingdom) was built... and it was marvellous. All creation marvelled that God the Son would stoop to take on humanity and allow Himself to be cursed, spat upon and put to death by His own creation... all for the sake of buying them back to make a people of God, drawn from every nation. WOW!!

Well, the chief priests and Pharisees understood Jesus' analogies perfectly... and they were not impressed. Rather than accept and learn from the rebuke, they sought all the more to get rid of Him.

READ MATTHEW 22: 1 – 14
How would you interpret this parable? [Luke 14: 15 – 24 may assist].

_____

_____

_____

_____

_____

_____

Revelation 19: 6 – 9 speaks of a wedding supper of the Lamb (Jesus) and His bride (the saints i.e. the church). Verse 9 says, "Blessed are those who are invited". Isaiah 24 prophesies the future judgment of the world and Isaiah 25: 6 – 8 tells of the feast that God will prepare when death is swallowed up forever. From the passage in Luke we see that the Jews knew there would be this feast in the kingdom of God. That is because they are the ones invited – they had the Old Testament Law and Prophets telling them all about Messiah and what He would bring. Jesus' charge against them in these passages was that when the invitation went out to them to come and share in the kingdom and its celebrations, they missed it. In fact, in Jamaica we would say they *"dissed it"* (they looked down on it, disregarded it, "disrespected" the honour of it). So others from the other nations, Gentiles, were welcomed in with open arms.

However, all who came to the banquet had to be properly attired in the appropriate "wedding clothes". This meant that regardless of which

- 159 -

nation you came from, everybody at the feast had to be "robed" in the blood of the Lamb, clothed in righteousness. The invitation goes out to all but only those who accept the conditions (salvation through the sacrifice of Jesus) comprised the chosen.

READ MATTHEW 22: 15 – 22
I have to laugh. Can you see His enemies shamefacedly slinking away, with "their tails between their legs"? Don't test!

READ LUKE 20: 27 – 40
The Sadducees, despite joining together with the Pharisees out of necessity (in attempting to discredit and trap Jesus), now used the opportunity to score their own points. They only accepted the Pentateuch (the first five books of the Old Testament) and rejected the other Old Testament writings; and they believed there was no resurrection. They thought the example they brought to Jesus proved irrefutably that there could not possibly be a resurrection. Jesus exposes their error and ignorance of the Scriptures: the resurrection life would not be the same as this life. There would be no more marrying and no more dying.

One is struck by the patience and graciousness of Jesus. He could have cited reasons from other places in the Old Testament but instead He chose to base His argument in the very book of Moses – the only section that they would accept. Thus He explains – if the Lord called Himself the God of Abraham, Isaac and Jacob (patriarchs long dead when He introduced Himself to Moses), and He is the God of the living not the dead; it meant that these patriarchs were alive in Him. The present life is not all there is; there is life after death. The Pharisees of course were pleased with this rebuttal [vs. 39].

READ MARK 12: 28 – 34
Matthew's gospel added that "All the law and the prophets hang on these two commandments". In other words, every other rule or command flows out of these two. Think about it. Doesn't it make sense? If you love God, you will desire to please Him and will therefore obey Him. Because

you love Him, you will also love others and would cause no hurt or harm to them.

The teacher of the law who asked this question seemed to be asking in earnest and not for the sake of trapping Jesus. His assertion that following these commands was more important than burnt offerings and sacrifices proved that he understood that God was not after works (external expressions of obedience), but after the condition of our hearts. Hence Jesus' declaration that he was not far from the kingdom of God.

READ MARK 12: 35 – 37
What was Jesus' point? _____
_____
_____
_____

READ MARK 12: 38 – 44
What lessons do we learn here? _____
_____
_____
_____
_____

Though it is true that the Christ would be a descendant (son) of David, the fact that David called Him Lord showed that He would be superior to him; in fact, his Lord. Messiah was God and man. He then went on to encourage them to not be caught up in the externals, like the Pharisees, who were robbing widows while professing holiness and perfection. A more comprehensive warning is given in Matthew chapter 23. What a contrast? These showy teachers of the law versus the poor widow who, though not giving much compared to those who had plenty, gave abundantly out of the little she had... true godliness.

I know it may appear that we are jumping all over the place, but really we have been looking at Jesus' teachings since His triumphal entry. I have endeavoured to select the testimonies that gave the most comprehensive recollection. Have you noticed that His teachings now focused on the future judgment and making oneself ready for it? He repeatedly explained what God, not man is looking at?

Write your prayer here:

CHAPTER 26

THE END OF THE AGE

Biblical prophecy, though always very accurate, can be confusing and overwhelming. As a result of this, many of us shy away from trying to understand it. We just read it and move on. However, the fact that God has taken the time to grant us a peek into what is to come indicates that it is important for us to know – whether to warn or encourage us.

One of the reasons prophecy can be confusing is that oftentimes two events are "compressed" into one prophecy. Thus, in the Old Testament, we read where the prophet would declare something that would happen to Israel in the relatively near future; and in the same breath continue to speak of something regarding a more distant time, either concerning the first coming of Messiah or the end times surrounding His second coming. This is called 'telescoping' – compressing two widely spaced events and seeing them together.

I believe this occurs because, while we are restricted to time and space, God has no such limitation. What we see as occurring presently and then ten years later, God sees as all occurring in His 'now'. The prophet (eg. Isaiah or Elijah) was often caught up in the spirit and in that state his physical senses were suspended and he would see as God sees – without the usual reference to chronological time. Note Isaiah 9:6 and the use of the present tense... for an event to occur 600 – 700 or more years later. This is why God knows our end from the beginning i.e. from before our lives begin; He already sees and knows its end and every second in between. Therefore, when God inspires the prophet to speak or write, He starts speaking of a future event and, especially when that event involves someone or something that reflects another more distant occurrence, He moves right into foretelling that later event also. As an example, the prophet Daniel has astounded many because many of his prophecies have already come to pass with striking accuracy. In Daniel 11, the prophet gives amazing detail of what would (and subsequently did) occur in the Greek Empire. At verse 21, he speaks of a "contemptible person that had not been given the honour of royalty". This, and all that he wrote down to verse 35 has been recognized as depicting Antiochus IV Epiphanes, who seized power while the rightful heir to the throne was still quite young.[14] However, verses 36 – 45 do not pertain to Antiochus and does not line up with what history has shown to be true of him. Many bible students believe that this is because the evil of Antiochus compares well with the future Antichrist that Revelation speaks of. Antiochus IV Epiphanes is thus considered a foreshadowing or 'type' of the Antichrist, and God therefore 'compressed' some of the events surrounding the Antichrist into those surrounding Antiochus, and inspired Daniel to record it.

Now, let us continue our study looking at Jesus' prophetic utterances surrounding the end times.

READ MATTHEW 24: 1 – 35
- What was Jesus referring to in verse 2? _____
- What three questions did the disciples ask Jesus in verse 3?

_____

_____

READ REVELATION 6: 1 – 14
- What do you think the first horseman depicts?

_____

- What power does the rider on the red horse have? _____

_____

- What do you think the third horseman indicates [look at vs. 6]?

_____

- What power does the fourth horseman have? _____
_____
- Who are we told about in verses 9 – 11? _____
- List the events that follow the opening of the sixth seal:

_____

_____

_____

_____

_____

Now, return to MATTHEW 24: -
- Do you see any similarity in this and what we just read in Revelation 6? _____
- If so, which verses in Matthew 24 correlate with Revelation 6? _____
_____

As Jesus and His disciples were leaving the temple, the disciples drew His attention to the magnificence of the temple structures. Jesus then prophesied that the entire thing would be torn down so that not even one stone would be left on another. This was fulfilled in AD 70 when Jerusalem was completely destroyed by the Romans. They even pulled apart the stones of the temple to get at the gold that had melted in between them when the temple had been set ablaze.

The disciples therefore asked Jesus three questions, arising out of His prophetic declaration:

1. When is the destruction going to occur;
2. What is the sign of His coming; and
3. What is the sign of the end of the age?

I suspect they recalled Daniel 9: 20 – 27, and hence their questions.

In responding, Jesus blends the answers to all three into one continuous monologue. When we look at Revelation 6, we meet the four horsemen of the Apocalypse. Looking at them in sequence, we see first a rider on a white horse, wearing a crown and riding out to conquer. Some have seen this as a figure of Christ because of the white horse. Others see it as the Antichrist and I am more inclined to agree with this latter position for a number of reasons.

Revelation 19: 11 – 16 gives a description of a rider on a white horse but goes into a detailed description which leaves no doubt that this is Christ – He is called Faithful and True; He is not just bent on conquest, but judges with justice; on His head are **many** crowns, not just one; and we are told that His name is the Word of God [recall Chapter 1 of our study]. We are left with no question as to who this rider is.

Contrast this with the first horseman in Revelation 6. Though he is on a white horse, he has only one crown and he only desires to conquer. I believe he is on a white horse because he is coming to deceive, to have people believe he is the Christ, but really he is the Antichrist. Comparing the sequence of events in Revelation 6 to that in Matthew 24, in my opinion, also confirms this. Let me explain.

In Revelation, the false Christ is released first (the rider on the white horse), bent on conquest. This is followed by the rider on the red horse, who was given power to remove peace from the earth and cause men to kill each other. In other words, the next sign would be the occurrence of wars. This is then followed by the rider on the black horse who clearly represents famine, a natural consequence of war. Thus we see in verse 6 how expensive basic food items would become. Next comes the rider on the pale horse whose name makes it clear what he represents – death and the grave. People on earth would therefore be killed by war, famine, plague, and devoured by wild animals. All this correlates very well with Matthew 24: 4 – 8, where the first sign Christ mentions is the appearing of false Christs, coming to deceive many. He also lists the wars, famine and earthquakes.

Verses 9 – 14 of Matthew goes on to describe believers being martyred for their faith, with some falling away and many being deceived. The ones who remain steadfast will be saved. This correlates with the scene in Revelation 6: 9 – 11 where we see the martyrs crying out for justice. It would appear then that Matthew 24: 4 – 14 is answering the question "What are the signs of the end of the age?". In fact, Jesus lets them know in verse 8 "… these are the beginning of birth pains". Think about labour pains – they start off fairly weak and widely spaced but get progressively stronger and ultimately more uncomfortable, unpleasant and frequent. Think about that.

Revelation 6: 12 – 15 very clearly reflects Matthew 24: 29 – 31, and Jesus precedes it in verses 26 – 28 by assuring His disciples that when the Son of Man comes, it will be as clear and visible as lightning in the skies, and as vultures seen circling over a carcass. They will not have to depend on word of mouth. Jesus therefore answered their question "What will be the sign of Your coming?" in Matthew 24: 26 – 35. Doesn't it all sound very frightening? Wars, earthquakes, and plagues … and then it gets worse. The sun and moon are darkened, meteors (stars) falling from the sky … can you picture the ensuing panic?

This leaves Matthew 24: 15 – 25 and, though placed seamlessly in between the signs of the end of the age and of His coming, appears to answer the third question regarding the destruction of the temple. The reference to the prophet Daniel in verse 15 relates to Daniel 9: 25 – 27. I believe the reason the answer comes in between the others is an example of what I referred to at the beginning of this chapter, i.e. 'telescoping'. The original reference in Daniel of "the abomination that causes desolation" is believed to refer to the attack on Jerusalem by Antiochus IV Epiphanes and the erection of a statue of Zeus in the Jerusalem temple. However, Jesus refers to it here as a reference to the destruction of Jerusalem and the temple in AD 70, and, some believe, to a future event in which the Antichrist will set up his image in Jerusalem [c.f. 2 Thessalonians 2: 1 – 4]. Thus all these events, because of their striking similarities, though separated by centuries, are thought to be compressed into one prophetic utterance.

So Christ will return and "gather His elect from the four winds, from one end of the heavens to the other". This concurs with what is written in 1 Thessalonians 4: 16 – 17. Notice how the bible interprets itself? Be aware, however, that others may interpret these prophecies very differently. My advice is to look into it and seek, by the guidance of the Spirit, the answers for yourself.

Memory verse: Matthew 24: 30 – 31.

READ MATTHEW 24: 36 – 44
- Who is the only one who knows the time of Christ's return? _____

  _____

- What do you think Jesus was saying in verse 37 – 41?

  _____

  _____

  _____

- What do you understand the charge to "keep watch" to mean? _____

  _____

  _____

READ MATTHEW 24: 45 – 51
- What is the lesson here? _____

  _____

  _____

I found it amazing that not even the Son of God Himself, knows exactly when the time of the end will be – only God the Father alone knows. Verses 37 – 41 let us know that it will come unexpectedly, while life is going on as usual. Verses 40 – 41 lend credence to the belief in the 'rapture', where believers are caught up to meet Jesus at His coming. The study of end time events is much greater than the scope of this present study, but is one I highly recommend, not in an effort to predict the when but to encourage us and prepare us for the what. Indeed, the charge given by Jesus to "keep watch" is not so much to look for the event of His coming, but more to remain in a state of readiness for it, *whenever* it should occur.

Hence the warning in verses 45 – 51. Notice that it was a warning to the Master's servant i.e. to the believer. It is not to the unbeliever who does not call Him Lord. In particular, that servant who has been given the stewardship of other believers (the Master's household) needs to ensure that they are found faithful and true to the task assigned when the Master returns. God holds those placed in positions of leadership over His sheep to a greater degree of accountability; and if verse 51 is true, "im no ramp!" (He doesn't play/romp i.e. He doesn't take it lightly). Remain steadfast to the end.

So friends, Jesus' last week clothed in human flesh is drawing to a close. His lessons have moved away from what God intended and expects of us, to what God will do. Like a good leader, He is preparing His followers for what they will face after He leaves … and not only His immediate disciples, but those of us who would come to follow Him out of their witness and testimony.

What do you want to say to God now?

CHAPTER 27

THE HOUR DRAWS CLOSER

Jesus continued His teaching – the Olivet Discourse (so named because He was on the Mount of Olives) – in Matthew 25. He told the parable of the 10 virgins awaiting the bridegroom who was a very long time in coming. The message again is remaining in a state of readiness despite the long wait. Those who were ready were able to join the feast.

We already looked at a similar lesson to the parable of the talents (Matthew 25: 14 – 30) in Chapter 23 when we studied Luke 19: 11 – 27. Therefore, we will now focus on the teaching on the sheep and goats.

READ MATTHEW 25: 31 – 46
- What is the setting? _____
  _____
- Who do the sheep represent? _____
- Who do the goats represent? _____
- What did the Lord count as kindness shown to Him? _____
  _____
- What was the final destination of those who had not shown concern?
  _____

The setting is clear from the passage – this is the final judgment when **all** nations – Jews and Gentiles, believers and unbelievers – are gathered before the throne. Note that it is Jesus, the Son of Man who is seated on this throne as King. It is not God the Father because verse 34 tells us the King says to the sheep on his right, "Come, you who are blessed by **my Father**…". The other thing I notice is that this is not a parable; Jesus is telling them exactly what would happen when He comes with His angels.

Another point that stands out for me is the fact that the inheritance/kingdom that was theirs had been prepared since the world was created. This reminds us again that it is humanity, not God, who is subject to time and space. From before creation until eternity to come – all of it is in God's present. Did you notice that the criteria for being declared righteous was not just being saved? It includes demonstrating that salvation in loving and caring for those in need. It was not works being done for commendation, to please Jesus and to ensure their salvation because we notice that they couldn't identify when it was they had shown care and concern to Jesus. They had simply gone about doing good.

It brings to mind Galatians 5: 66, "The only thing that counts is faith expressing itself through love." Do not make the mistake of believing that it was their works that saved them. Read Ephesians 2: 8 – 10. It is not our works that save us, it is faith; but we were re-created in Christ Jesus to do good works. Someone has said it this way – we work out what Christ has worked in [us].

Some have suggested that Jesus' use of the words "brothers of mine" means He was referring to the Jews. However, the Greek word used for brothers is "adelphos" and seems therefore to be speaking of mankind, not just the Jewish people. The passage demonstrates well the two greatest commandments which really form the basis of all other commandments: Love God, and love each other.

Those not deemed righteous were sent into hell (the eternal fire) – think about that – **eternal** fire. The modern day philosophy is that we should avoid all references to hell as individuals opt to deny its existence. "How could a loving God create such a wicked place for mankind?" is the question asked. The fact is, however, that ignoring it won't make it go away – there really is such a place; but it was not created for mankind, it was created for the rebellious angels who sought to overthrow God. Those of mankind who end up there choose to follow the rebellion of the devil and his cohorts, and so place themselves under the same punishment.

Wednesday

READ LUKE 21: 37 – 22: 6
I had us read this i) to see the flow of events, and ii) to recognize Satan's role. We know the plot was set in place on Wednesday, because Matthew 26: 1 – 2 tells us the Passover was two days away.

READ JOHN 12: 20 – 36
- Of what nationality were the seekers mentioned here? _____
- Summarize Jesus' response in verses 23 – 26 _____

- What does it mean to follow Jesus?

- What do you think He meant by
  a. "the time for judgment on this world"? _____

  b. "the prince of this world will be driven out"? _____

It may come as a surprise to some of us to see that it was not only Jews who had come to the feast. Gentiles also came to worship and here we meet some Greeks who had obviously heard about Jesus and wanted to see Him. I love that. How many of us have longed to see Jesus? For some reason this caused Jesus to declare that "His time" had finally come. All the previous times where we saw the Jewish leaders and crowd trying to kill Him, they couldn't because "His time had not yet come". Now, it had. Was it because that message was now spreading beyond the borders of Israel to the rest of the world, so that other nations were now seeking Him? Was it because both Jew and Gentile would be present to see Him pay the just penalty due for their sins? Regardless, know it was no easy task to even look forward to, and we are allowed a glimpse into the turmoil in His heart in verse 27. Despite the "butterflies in His stomach" regarding what He would soon endure, He refused to turn away from His destiny. Instead, He asked the Father to glorify His Name.

In the context of surrendering His life so that we might live, His statement that those who serve Him must follow Him suggests to me that we too are called to lay down our lives – that is what it means to follow Him. Indeed, the root meaning of 'disciple' includes submitting to the principle of being willing to die, if necessary, for the sake of the rabbi whose life and teaching were being adhered to. Are we, His disciples in this present day, willing to die for Jesus' sake? We might not be hung on a tree/cross, but we are called to count our lives (our plans, our rights, our way) dead. Someone has said that the problem with a living sacrifice is that it keeps crawling off the altar. We are called to stay put; to be "walking dead", so to speak. Think about that.

The crowd (likely, including these Greeks) heard the manifestation of God's voice thundering from heaven. Jesus then confirmed that it was time for judgment on this world i.e. the due penalty for all our sins would be paid shortly. The judgment rendered was a guilty verdict and the sentence laid down was death by crucifixion. The result would be the loosening of the power Satan (the prince of this world) held over mankind. Thus he would be driven out. Jesus' crucifixion would free both Jew and Gentile, paving the way to draw us all to Him.

READ JOHN 12: 37 – 41

The writer of John lets us know that Isaiah saw it all centuries before, and recorded his vision. We will take a closer look at that prophecy in a later chapter.

READ JOHN 12: 42 – 50

Think about what you have just read.

We will be judged for ignoring what we heard God say, because having heard, we are responsible for what we do with it.

BRINGING IT HOME:
Has the Lord called you to a position of leadership in His body? Leaders do not have an easy task, especially those serving in the Kingdom. It is not always easy to get others to follow especially if they have their own ideas about what should be done, despite what the leader believes the Lord is saying to do. It can be an overwhelming and often thankless task. Take heart, friend – do not be weary in well-doing; you will receive the Lord's blessing.
Are you a believer, a follower of Christ? In light of what we studied today, have you accepted that you are to be a living sacrifice, 'dying daily' – deliberately and without hesitation as an act of pure worship to God? How can you demonstrate that in everyday life?

PRAYER: -

Father, it is so easy to lose sight of things eternal in the daily happenings of life. Help me to not get so caught up in the peripherals – the things that seem important and urgent now but tomorrow are not even remembered. Help me to focus on that which will remain beyond this life. I confess some feelings of anxiety when I think of following You in laying down my life, but the truth is it was never mine to begin with – I am Yours. Nothing I could plan or want for myself could ever exceed or even compare to what You plan for me. You know me better than I know myself, and I do believe I will find fulfillment only in Your plan and purpose. Open my eyes to see that purpose, Lord, and walk faithfully in it. Thank You, gracious God, for Your patience with me.

CHAPTER 28

THE LAST SUPPER

Thursday

The synoptic gospels give a different focus from that in John's gospel, of the last Passover Supper that Jesus shared with His disciples. The latter gospel recounts an extensive discourse where Jesus prepares, teaches and prays for His disciples. On the other hand, the synoptics focus primarily on the meal and Jesus' institution of the Last Supper.

READ LUKE 22: 7 – 13, then JOHN 13: 1 – 17

1. What was the day called [Luke 22: 7]? _____

2. Which two disciples were sent to make the preparations for the meal?
   _____

3. What do you understand John 13: 3 & 4 to be saying? _____
   _____

4. Discuss Jesus' statement: "Unless I wash you, you have no part with Me." _____
   _____
   _____
   _____

5. What was the lesson that Jesus was teaching His disciples in this passage in John's gospel? _____
   _____
   _____

It is significant to me that it was Peter and John, the two disciples who followed (albeit at a distance) and stayed during His trial and subsequent crucifixion (as we will later see), who prepared the Passover lamb for that last supper. John lets us know that while the meal was being served, Jesus – who knew His authority and was secure in the knowledge of who He was – proceeded to practically illustrate that true leadership is demonstrated in humility and service. In fact, I think He was showing them that no task was too menial to do for each other. That is in fact love. The common practice was that invited guests would have their feet washed by a servant when they entered the house. None of the disciples had seen to this because it was considered a servant's task. Jesus, despite knowing He was Lord over all, chose to be the servant to His disciples. For Him, it was no humiliation; rather, it was a demonstration of His love, and a precursor to the ultimate expression of that love … dying on the cross (the full extent of his love).

That act of supreme sacrifice would also bring about our "washing" in His blood and thus cleansing from sin. Without that "washing", we cannot become a part of his body [John 13: 8] – we would have no part with Him. I suspect that though Jesus was referring to the washing of His disciples' feet, it also referred to what was to come in terms of the cross. Jesus encouraged His disciples to follow His example – don't lord it over each other – rather, serve one another. We have met this instruction before.

READ LUKE 22: 14 – 23
1. What do you believe Jesus meant in verse 16? _____
2. How many cups are mentioned in this passage? _____
3. What kind of bread was used here? _____
4. What did Jesus say it represented? _____
5. What did the second cup mentioned represent? _____

To fully understand the significance of this Supper and Jesus' declaration of a "new covenant" in His blood, it helps to have an appreciation of what Passover represented and the stages of the Passover celebration.

READ EXODUS 12: 1 – 20

As a background, the Israelites had been made slaves in Egypt and the Lord God had sent Moses to deliver them from this bondage under Pharaoh. God had already sent a number of plagues upon Egypt but Pharaoh kept resisting God's demand to let His people go, disregarding God and insisting that this God was no greater than the gods of Egypt. Almighty God, therefore, decreed a final plague: He would pass through Egypt and kill every firstborn male – human and animal, and thus bring judgment on all the gods of Egypt [Exo. 12: 12].

From this passage,

1. What animal was to be sacrificed and eaten? _____

_____

2. What were the stipulations about the type of animal? _____

_____

3. What were the Israelites to do with the blood of the sacrifice? _____

_____

4. What kind of bread was to be eaten? _____

_____

5. What effect would the blood on the houses have? _____

_____

6. From verses 15 – 20, what was an important part of the celebration?

_____

Thus the blood of a spotless, unblemished lamb (one without defect), painted over the entrances to the dwellings of the Israelites was the sign to the destroyer to "pass over" the inhabitants of that dwelling, and not carry out the sentence of death there. That is why the celebration to commemorate this was called the Passover.

Returning then to the passage in Luke, and examining the stages of the Passover feast, let us see if we can get a better understanding of what Jesus was saying to His disciples. Recall that Peter and John had to make preparations for the feast. This would have included preparing the sacrificed lamb and getting the room ready, but would also mean getting unleavened bread i.e. bread made without yeast (yeast being symbolic of sin/evil – c.f. 1Corinthians 5: 6 – 8 & Matt. 16: 6 & 12). Thus, in the week leading up to the feast, all yeast is removed from the dwelling, symbolic of separating oneself from sin and unto God. For the Jews this was part of the Kiddush (sanctification), the first part of the Passover.

The whole ceremony is called the Pesach or Passover Seder (order). During this they fill a small cup or small wine glass with wine at four different points in the Seder and drink each cup of wine. These four cups of Passover relate to the four "I wills" in **Exodus 6: 6 – 7** (read). In Luke 22: 16 when Jesus said, "…until it finds fulfillment in the kingdom", He was indicating that the Passover was just a foreshadowing of what He came to do. His upcoming sacrificial death on the cross to bear our sins, and covering us in His blood was the fulfillment of what Passover had really always represented. When He took the first cup mentioned in verse 17, this is believed to be the first cup of the Passover, the cup of Sanctification, relating to the first "I will" i.e. "bring you out from the yoke of Egypt". This was followed by the ritual washing of the hands – all a picture of sanctification. There are some who believe that it is at this point in the Seder that Jesus may have washed His disciples' feet.

Here too, among other things, would be the breaking of the middle Matzah (unleavened bread) i.e. "sinless" bread; symbolizing Jesus, the bread of life, sinless; broken for us. Imagine what it must have meant to the disciples when He broke it and said it really represented His body that would be given for them [Luke 22: 19]. When this is broken, one piece is wrapped in white cloth and hidden away, to be found after the meal. Do you see the correlation to Jesus' death and subsequent burial?

The second cup, the cup of Judgment would be drunk just **before** the main meal, and represented "I will deliver you from slavery". It is so named because it commemorates the judgment passed on the Egyptians: lives were sacrificed to bring about release from slavery. (One cannot help but see an association to Jesus, our "Passover lamb", being sacrificed to release us from bondage to sin). It is a cup of rejoicing. This is followed by the Passover supper which included lamb, unleavened bread and bitter herbs. After the meal, the piece of Matzah that was wrapped and hidden is found (resurrected?). In Passover, no food is eaten after this.

After supper [Luke 22: 20], the third cup – the cup of **Redemption** – is drunk… representing His blood poured out for us. Here, Jesus opened their eyes to a new covenant. To understand this, look at Exodus 24: 3 – 8: here is the old covenant confirming Israel's commitment to follow the Law. However, in Jeremiah 31: 31 – 34, we see God promising a new covenant and then, in Luke, Jesus institutes that new covenant. The fourth cup – of Praise or Restoration – is drunk after the conclusion of the "Hallel" where Psalm 136: 1 – 16 is recited. This is then followed by more praise.[151617]

Isn't it amazing? For centuries, the Jewish people would have been celebrating Passover in commemoration of God's miraculous deliverance from bondage in Egypt; yet all the time this was looking forward to Jesus' selfless sacrifice delivering us from bondage to sin. Now, when we celebrate the Lord's Supper, we celebrate this deliverance from sin and the just penalty – death. Oh, what a love!

READ JOHN 13: 18 – 30
Jesus was not unaware of His betrayer. Though He had washed all His disciples, He knew that one of them still did not remain a part of Him… and He let the disciples know it so that they would not be questioning themselves after His death. He let them know so that it would help to strengthen their faith when they needed it most. There is another lesson in this. *You can fool others and even yourself, but you cannot fool God. You can go to church, be involved in all kinds of religious activities, be considered the most super-spiritual Christian, but God knows who really belong to Him. Read 2 Timothy 2: 19!* Are you really a part of His body?

READ LUKE 22: 24 – 38
We again are privy to another testimonial of Jesus encouraging His disciples to see themselves as servant leaders – a Kingdom principle that is in sharp contradistinction to the world's principle. Did you notice that

He conferred on them positions of rulership [verses 28 – 30]? Given the context, this appears to be a promise for the future.

BRAATA : -

It is a common misconception that when Christ returns, we who are believers will be taken up to live in Heaven and do nothing but feast on milk and honey, play harps and gaze into the face of Jesus, the One we love. However, based on what the Word of God says, there will be a new Heaven and a new Earth; and a New Jerusalem that will come down out of heaven so that the dwelling of God will be with men [Revelation 21]. Those who believed in Jesus will reign with Him on the Earth [Revelation 5: 9 – 10]. Recall what we read in Luke 19: 11 – 27, in Chapter 22 of this study: the servants who had gained an interest on the Mina invested in them, were placed in charge of cities. What are your thoughts on this?

What did Jesus tell Simon? _____

_____

What do you think this meant? _____

_____

What did Jesus instruct him to do? _____

_____

Why do you think Jesus gave them different instructions in verse 36?

_____

_____

Jesus continues to encourage and prepare His closest followers. Judas would have missed all of what Christ told the other disciples after the meal, based on what we read in John 13: 30. It is not lost on me that Jesus pointed out that they had remained faithful and stayed with Him throughout all the opposition and accusations He had faced thus far. They had endured to the end. I believe that it is this that made them worthy of receiving a kingdom, and afforded them an invitation to sit at His table. Child of God, what are the implications of this in your life? Are you prepared to stand in the midst of persecution, questioning, disappointment, etc.? If Jesus returned now, would you be counted worthy of receiving a kingdom?

The Lord then warns them that Satan has requested the chance to test them; to see if they are really true [for a similar event, see Job chapters 1 & 2]. (As an aside, what could we infer from this?). Please note that, though Jesus addressed Simon Peter, the word "you" in vs. 31 is plural. In other words, Jesus was telling Peter that Satan had asked permission to test all of them, but He had prayed for the strengthening of Peter's faith and was encouraging him to strengthen the others, when he had repented and returned (after failing). What do we learn here?

Don't we all, like Peter, often overestimate our strength? Isn't it good to know that God knows us better than we know ourselves and, despite knowing our short-comings, loves us unwaveringly?

We round off this session taking note of the fact, that, whereas before Jesus had instructed the disciples to "take no thought" about their needs in going out and spreading the gospel; now, He warns them to ensure they had not just all they needed, but also instructs them to prepare to defend themselves. I believe He did so because He knew that they would now be entering a time of persecution arising out of His upcoming trial and death.

What thoughts cross your mind as you meditate on these things? Bring them to God in prayer now.

CHAPTER 29

IN THE UPPER ROOM

Judas had left; and Jesus continued to speak to His friends.

READ JOHN 13: 31 – 38

- What do you think it means to be glorified? _____
  _____
- Verses 31 & 32 may seem quite confusing. Read it again, and write
  what you think it is saying. _____
  _____
  _____
- How will the world be able to identify Christ's followers? _____
  _____
- Is this true of you? _____

The Greek word translated "glorify" is *"doxazo"*. Vine's tells us this means
" to magnify, extol, praise". Especially when used as "glorifying God", it
means to ascribe honour to Him, acknowledging Him as to His being,
attributes and acts. The glory of God is the revelation and manifestation
of all that He has and is. When it is through Christ that this is made
evident, He is said to glorify the Father [18]. Isn't it interesting then that
upon Judas' departure (which sets into motion the events that will lead
ultimately to the cross), Jesus calls this the time of His being glorified;
and God being glorified in Him? This is because Jesus was about to
demonstrate who He really was, Messiah, and was about to demonstrate

God's love by submitting to die on a cross in obedience to His Father, bringing us out of bondage to sin and death. Thus God would also be glorified as love personifed. In other words, what the world would see as the ultimate defeat was really the greatest triumph! A friend saw it as God's final vindication – man could willingly return in humble submission to God, through faith in Jesus Christ. God's original will and purpose would be realized, as all would be submitted to Him, and God **alone and unchallenged** would be all in all [1 Corinth. 15: 28].

Isn't it tragic, though, that we (the church) are so self-consumed that the love that we ought to be demonstrating to and for each other, the love that should be a reflection of the love of Christ and the Father, is often lacking or over-shadowed by our petty grievances and insistence on our own rights. When indeed will we really love each other and exhibit to the world the evidence of Christ in us?!

READ JOHN 14: 1 – 14
Having already heard that one of them would betray Him, the disciples were then told by Jesus that He would be leaving them shortly; and to make matters worse, they couldn't go where He was going [vs. 33]. On top of that, He informed Peter of his impending denial. You can literally feel the depression filling that upper room. What a letdown after the excitement of the triumphant entry into Jerusalem a few days previously. The Lord therefore encouraged them – they would see Him again, but first He needed to go and prepare a place for them.

- Where was He referring to when He said that? _____
- Then, what is He saying when He states that He is the way, etc.? ___
  _____
  _____
  _____
  _____

In Isaiah 66: 1, the Lord says: "Heaven is My throne, and the earth is My footstool." Jesus, therefore, was telling His disciples that He was returning to His Father in Heaven. He then made the 7th "I AM" statement found in the gospel of John: "I am the way and the truth and the life. No one comes to the Father except through Me."

Stop and think about that statement. Jesus never said that He was **a** way; rather, He was **the** way.

The way to somewhere usually indicates the path or the means to get there. This emphatic statement by Jesus declares that He is the *ONLY* way to the Father and heaven; He is the *ONLY* truth (truth has to be absolute, or it is not truth, it is opinion); and in Him *ALONE* is life, eternal life. The statement "No one comes to the Father except through Me" leaves NO room for alternatives! We cannot eliminate the passages of scripture that we may disagree with – take it or leave it, *"a so it go!"* (that's how it is!). This throws out the notion that there are many paths that lead to God.

- From verses 7 – 11, what do you understand about the relationship between Jesus and the Father? [Recall what Jesus said in John 10: 30].

  _____

  _____

- Any comments on verses 12 – 14? _____

  _____

  _____

  _____

This "oneness" that existed between Jesus and the Father permeates Jesus' every word and action. All He said and all He did were governed by the Father in Him. Thus, even the miracles He did, Jesus gives the credit to the Father in Him. But Jesus went further to declare that all of us who have faith in Him will do the same. I believe this is because those of us who believe in Him become a part of His body and therefore one with Him … and therefore one with the Father also.

Moreover, with Jesus' departure back to heaven, the Holy Spirit – the One who knows the mind and heart of God [1 Corinthians 2: 11 – 12] – would be deposited in us. We therefore would be privy to the heart and mind of God, through this Holy Spirit. We would therefore be in a position to ask for anything, *according to the will, nature and character of God*. Obviously, if we ask in this way, it will be done because it is according to His will.

Do not for one second fall prey to this doctrine of "name it and claim it", insisting it is yours because you tagged on the line "in the Name of Jesus". The aim is to bring glory to the Father so as we pray in Jesus' Name, we are praying according to the character and nature of Jesus. Notice that nothing Jesus did was for Himself; it was according to the will of the Father and for His glory.

READ JOHN 14: 15 – 31
Write down your insights here.

_____

_____

_____

_____

Jesus again reiterates that our love for Him will be demonstrated in our obedience to Him. What He goes on to say regarding the Counselor (the Holy Spirit) confirms what we said earlier: He will reveal to us the truth [vs. 17] and so lets us know God's heart and will.

Have you noticed the complete "interconnectedness" of the Father, the Son and the Holy Spirit? Jesus said He was going to the Father but would ask the Father who would send another Counselor (Jesus being the first one), the Holy Spirit. Yet He goes on to say in verse 18 that He wouldn't leave the disciples as orphans; He (Jesus would come to them and though the world wouldn't see Him anymore, the disciples would. Verse 20 clinches it: Jesus would be in the Father, the disciples (and believers) would be in Him (we are His body), **and** He would be **in** us. How? Through the Holy Spirit.

So we see oneness not just of the Father and the Son, but of the Holy Spirit as well. This is why we speak of a Triune God or Godhead. Verse 23 further confirms this. We have already seen that the Holy Spirit would be in us [vs. 17]. Now verse 23 says that those who love and obey Him

(Jesus), i.e. believers, would also have the "plural" God (Three in One) come to them and dwell in them (note the use of the words – "*we* will come to him and make *our* home with him"). Jesus explains to Judas (son of James, also called Thaddaeus) that this is why the world (those who do not believe) will not see Him (Jesus): the Godhead will not invade (enter without invitation) those who do not love and obey Him.

- What functions of the Holy Spirit are mentioned in this passage? ___

_____

- What do you think is the difference between the world's peace and that which Jesus gives? _____

_____

_____

The prince of the world, Satan, would soon think he had triumphed – believing that killing the Son would ensure his taking over His inheritance. It reminds me of the parable of the tenants that we looked at in Matthew 21: 33 – 41. Though we already elaborated on its meaning, I can't help but wonder if Satan, who always desired to be God, thought that killing the heir would ensure his chances of that. Yet, all the while, no one could take Christ's life – He gave it up willingly, of his own accord, because He loved the Father; and to love was to obey.

BRINGING IT HOME: -
Do you really love the Lord?
Would the way you live your life right now prove it?
Is it a life of obedience to His will, no matter the cost or inconvenience?
Or is your obedience contingent on what you think makes practical sense?

PRAYER: -
Father, I confess that I don't always obey You. I take for granted too often, Your mercy and grace. I just go along thinking You will understand, and prefer to pretend that You understand that times have changed. But deep down, Lord, I know You do not change. Please forgive me, Lord, and teach me how to love the way You do.

CHAPTER 30

ON THE WAY TO GETHSEMANE

John chapters 13 – 17 have been called the Upper Room Discourse because it is thought to encompass some of Christ's most intimate teachings with His disciples from the Last Supper up to just before He is taken to be tried and crucified. However, the end of Chapter 14 suggests that Chapters 15 – 17 occurred while leaving the upper room and moving on their way to Gethsemane. It's not a vital point; just a recognition of the fact that He had said, "Come now, let us leave."

READ JOHN 15: 1 – 17
In this analogy of the vine,

1. Who are the branches? _____
2. What happens to the branches that do not produce fruit? _____
   _____
3. What happens to the ones that do? _____
4. What prerequisite to bearing fruit is stated here? _____
   _____
5. What happens to the ones that do not remain in the vine? _____
   _____

The first thing to note is that Jesus is speaking about those who are a part of Him since He uses the analogy of a vine and its branches. Therefore, He is not speaking about the people in the world, but rather those of us in the church. The NIV Bible states in John 15: 2 that "He cuts off every branch in Me that bears no fruit". The Greek word that means "to cut off" is "apokopto" and was used, for example, in Mark 9 where Jesus spoke of cutting off your hand or your foot, if they caused you to sin – pointing to the resolute attitude we should have about dealing with sin in our lives.

In John 15:2, however, the original Greek word is "airo" which means "to lift, carry, take up or away" [Vine's Complete Expository Dictionary], and some other translations of the Bible render that verse as "He takes away every branch..." which would seem more accurate. I point out the distinction as some commentators believe that rather than removing such branches, the Father lifts them up (as a gardener may do to a plant) so that they may be better able to bear fruit. Nevertheless, it should be noted that "airo" was also the word used when John the Baptist saw Jesus and declared in John 1: 29, "Look, the Lamb of God, who *takes away* the sins of the world!"

When we look at the entire passage, seeing the context, we will not be left confused. Jesus says in John 15: 5 that if we remain in Him *we will bear **much** fruit*. Putting it another way, you cannot be in Him and not bear fruit – fruit-bearing is a natural consequence of being a part of His Body. Therefore, whether one is lifted up so as to bear fruit, or taken away because of lack of fruit-bearing, God expects fruit! Those who are not bearing fruit are *not* remaining in Him. Still, those bearing fruit are pruned. Fruit-bearing does not spare you pain – God desires that you bear much fruit and will remove the dead 'leaves' and excess from your branch (the things that sap/reduce His life-giving flow to the important areas of your life) so that you produce kingdom crop.

Questions: -

i.   Are you bearing fruit? _____
ii. If you are, are there distractions and diversions that are reducing your spiritual 'energy' and preventing you from increasing your crop?

_____

iii. If so, what are these? _____

_____

_____

iv. Are you still in the vine, or are you withering away apart from Him?

_____

_____

Verse 6 makes it clear that you could at one time have been in the vine, but then cease to be. The treatment given to such a one is to be thrown into the fire. This passage makes us look closely at our lives as Christians. We have probably all heard the phrase "Once saved, always saved." Based on the passage in John and others (e.g. Hebrews 10: 26 – 39), it is clear that receiving Christ as Saviour but then proceeding to live a life apart from Him and producing no evidence of His life-giving blood in your life leaves you in no better position than those in the world. You are destined for the fire.

It is true that the Lord said, "…no one can snatch them out of My hand" [John 10: 25 – 29], but even in that context, Jesus was speaking of sheep that **listen** to His voice **and follow** Him. The true Christian demonstrates the out-working of Jesus in his life. I would therefore say it is more accurate to say, "Once truly saved, always saved". Similarly, the Greek says that those who are *continually* led by the Spirit of God are "sons of God" [Romans 8:14].

Notice again the prerequisite to answered prayer in vs. 7. It involves remaining in Jesus and allowing His words (His teachings and commands) to transform you as you obey them, understanding and following His will. As we demonstrate that we are God's children, He receives the glory (the praise and honour).

How are we to love each other? _____

How much did Christ love us? _____

When are we considered Christ's friends? _____

What is the friend privy to? _____

Jesus' command (not request) was to love each other *as He loved us* i.e. sacrificially and purposefully. We, like Him, should be willing to die for each other – that's the kind of love He commands. And He said that if we love Him, we would obey Him. When we become so self-less and so much more concerned about others, the Lord knows then that He can trust us with His secrets – we now become His friends, not just servants. *Then* God will give us whatever we ask in Jesus Name - according to the character of Jesus and by the rights invested in us by Him. This is akin to the rights which a wife has by virtue of her marriage, having legal access to all that is her husband's.

READ JOHN 15: 18 – 16: 4

Jesus now prepares His disciples for the upcoming persecution they will face. Jesus' statement in verse 22 stands out for me. Those who are ignorant will not be held accountable, but for those of us who have heard, we will be held responsible and accountable for what we know. We are without excuse.

- What have you done with what you have learnt from God's Word?
- Has it changed the way you think and the way you live?

Jesus declared that the Spirit would reveal to men's hearts the truth as to who Jesus is; and Jesus instructed His disciples to testify also about Him since they were there throughout His earthly ministry.

READ JOHN 16: 5 – 16

- What does the passage declare to be the work of the Holy Spirit in the world? _____

_____

_____

- What will He do for the disciples? _____

_____

Jesus seemed to be pointing out to the disciples that they were so consumed with grief at the thought of His leaving that they hadn't even asked Him where He was going. He wanted them to know that it was a good thing, so they should rejoice, not weep. After all, He was returning to His Father and they (the disciples) would have the Counselor with them; and His activity in the world and in them would be far-reaching.

As noted before, it is the Holy Spirit that convicts us of our sin, He lets us know and understand that we have missed the mark. It is He who draws us to Christ, to accepting, believing and laying hold of the salvation Jesus purchased for us – we cannot work to attain it. He also helps us to understand that there will be a time of judgment when the hearts of men are laid bare, and we will be held accountable for how we have lived. Again, it is the Holy Spirit that enables us to understand the word of God so that we come to know God.

READ JOHN 16: 17 – 33
- What do you think Jesus was referring to in verses 20 – 22? _____
  _____
- Why would the disciples no longer ask Jesus anything [vs. 23 – 24] & why would Jesus not ask the Father for anything on their behalf [vs. 26 – 27]? _____
  _____
  _____
  _____

While the world would rejoice at the death of Jesus, thinking they had killed a con-artist and blasphemer; the disciples would be grieving ... until the resurrection morning and the realization that death has no control over the Lord of the Universe. In that day, when sin and its power over us would be conquered, then would the disciples, and later we, have free access to the Father directly! No more would they need to ask Jesus; and no more would He have to be their spokesperson. In that day, the separation between God and man caused by sin would be removed by the blood of Jesus and His victory over death. God's original intention of having relationship with man would be restored.

Why, according to the passage, does God love the disciples [vs. 27]? ____
_____

It almost seems like God will move mountains for those who love and accept His Son, doesn't it? Jesus then puts it plainly for His disciples. He left His Father in Heaven and came to the world and would now be returning to God. Finally, the disciples got it! Despite this, fear would still cause them to scatter and leave Him alone. Yet, He knew that God's presence was with Him.

Memory verse: John 16: 33
"I have told you these things, so that in Me you may have peace. In this world you will have trouble. But take heart! I have overcome the world."

He never promised us a "bed of roses" or an easy ride; but He did promise victory!

PRAYER: -
Lord, so often You reveal things to me that challenge me to rethink and stop accepting what the world says to be true. Yet, at the same time, I may opt for the easier route of ignoring what I understood You to say, either because I'm so comfortable with the way things are or because I'm afraid of what others will think of me. Help me to be more concerned about what You think. Help me to see clearly and not settle for less than Your best for me.

CHAPTER 31

THE PRAYERS OF A RIGHTEOUS MAN

READ JOHN 17: 1 – 5
- Over what does Jesus have authority? _____
- What is eternal life? _____
- What does that mean to you? _____
  _____
  _____

- What do we learn about Jesus in vs. 4? _____
  _____
- How long has He existed? _____

READ JOHN 17: 6 – 19
- In vs. 6, who are "those who You gave Me"? _____
- What do we know about them based on Jesus' conclusion in verses
  6 – 8? _____
- What is Jesus' prayer for them? _____
- Do you have any thoughts as to what Jesus meant in vs. 12 when He
  said that He "kept them safe by that Name" that God gave Him?
  _____
  _____

- Who is the one "doomed to destruction"? _____
- Summarize verses 14 – 16 in your own words. _____
  _____
  _____

- The word 'sanctify' means to set apart, in this context unto God, for His use; to be made holy. What then do you think verse 17 is saying then? _____

_____

- What do you think Jesus means when He says that He sanctifies Himself that they may be truly sanctified? _____

_____

In John 17, we are given the awesome privilege of hearing exactly what Jesus prayed to His Father. Let me set the stage. By now night has fallen. Jesus has had His last meal earlier that evening. As stated before, I believe He and His disciples were moving toward Gethsemane. He knows the time is drawing nearer to His impending suffering and death. We are made privy to His thoughts, His concerns, and His feelings, as He faces this "death sentence".

He starts at the relationship between Himself and the Father. We see Him acquiescing to God demonstrating His power in and through Him. I believe this is what He is doing when He tells God to glorify Him so that God Himself may be glorified. In other words, He is lining up His will with the Father's, and surrendering to His fate. God will receive glory out of His Son's crucifixion. Why? Because He had been given the authority over *all* people to afford them the opportunity to have eternal life, by His death and resurrection. Still, only those who belong to Him would receive this eternal life. This makes sense since eternal life is knowing (having an intimate relationship with) God (the *only* real God there is [vs. 3]), and knowing (having an intimate relationship with) Jesus Christ i.e. believing in Him, accepting Him, allowing Him to govern your life, and becoming His bride. These individuals will not experience death (i.e. eternal separation from God) because they have a love relationship with Him.

Jesus brought glory to God by obeying Him to the end; He did what God had sent Him to do. (We also glorify God by obeying Him). As a result, Jesus would return to His place of authority in Heaven, in the Father's presence, that He had always possessed (from eternity, before the world was created). We see again evidence of His divinity.

Jesus then goes on to pray for His disciples. He confirms that they are true believers in Him, acknowledging Him to be Messiah. He prays for their protection as He will be leaving them; and that they may be *one, as He and the Father are one*. Think about that. How was the "oneness" of God and His Son demonstrated? That is the kind of oneness He desired for His disciples.

I spent some time meditating on verse 12, wondering what He meant when He said He had kept them safe "by that Name". Initially, Proverbs 18: 10 came to mind:

> "The Name of the Lord is a strong tower; the righteous run into it and are safe."

We therefore often think of the Lord's Name as a shield, an authority that when drawn upon, carries with it the weight of His power and sovereignty.

However, when we read from the Amplified version, we get a different interpretation that to me appears more accurate, given the context. It states:

> "While I was with them, I kept and preserved them **in** Your Name [in the knowledge and worship of You] ... and not one of them has perished or is lost except the son of perdition [Judas Iscariot]".

This suggests that Jesus was saying that while He was with them, He kept them faithful to God and believing, so they remained in Him, except for Judas Iscariot. The Living Bible puts it nicely:

> "During My time here I have kept safe **within Your family** all of these You gave Me. I guarded them so that not one perished, except the son of hell". Doesn't that seem clearer?

The disciples had received and accepted God's life-changing word which transformed them and, like Jesus made them different, and caused them to stand out from the world. Yet they still had to live in the world; so Jesus prayed for their protection. When one is sanctified, one is set apart *from* something and *to* something. The truth, the Word of God, had set the disciples apart from the world. They no longer fit into its way of life and thinking. At the same time, it had set them apart for God's use; His work. To enable them to truly accomplish this divine purpose placed on their lives, Jesus "set apart" Himself i.e. he let Himself be crucified so that His resurrection life in them, through the Holy Spirit, would enable them to fulfill the divine task for which they were set apart and made distinct.

READ JOHN 17: 20 – 26
- Who are those described in verse 20? _____

- What was Jesus' primary prayer to the Father regarding them? ____

- What would be the result of that? _____

Jesus' final prayer here was a prayer for us – those who would become believers because of the testimony of the disciples. He had us Christians on His mind; and He prayed, asking the Father that we would be one …in fact, that we be so united that we reflect the oneness of the Godhead! And this, **so that the world would believe in Jesus and know God's love**. This is the primary evangelism tool – the unity of the body of Christ. No wonder Satan has sought to divide us. The sad question is, "Why do we let him?"

Jesus declared that He has given us the glory that God gave Him. That means that we as Christians have the power and the authority of Christ resident in us and evidenced through the indwelling Holy Spirit! In fact, the whole power of the Godhead resides in us [vs. 23].

Pause here and think about the fact that the unity in the church, the body of Christ, is what will let others really believe in Jesus. What are the ways that we create divisions? How can we seek to mend them, while holding fast to the truth?

PRAYER: -

Father, help me to understand what it means to have You residing in me, with all the power, authority and love that You possess. Help me also to seek after unity in Your body. Let me not contribute to tearing apart Your body, limb by limb; but rather to help to heal and bring wholeness. May we indeed, show the world that You are real.

CHAPTER 32

EVIL REIGNS

Friday

We now come to the events of that fateful Friday. We will start in the "garden of Gethsemane", very early in the morning, long before daybreak. From the eyewitness accounts of His disciples, we will attempt to piece together the sequence of events as they occurred. Be warned! This is not for the faint-hearted.

READ MATTHEW 26: 36 – 46
- What is the overriding mood in this scene? _____
- Describe Jesus' state of mind. _____

_____

- What do you make of Jesus' rebuke and admonition to Peter and the disciples in vs. 41? _____

_____

Most of us have heard about the garden of Gethsemane. Luke tells us they went to the Mount of Olives, apparently a common practice of Jesus. John [NIV] tells us it was an olive grove. It is clear that the anxiety of His impending ordeal weighed heavily on Him. It does seem appropriate that His wrestling with and decisively submitting to God's will should occur in the place where oil is pressed out of olives (Gethsemane means "oil press").

The picture painted here leaves us with no doubt that Jesus was subject to all the weaknesses, fears, anxiety and pain that we all, as humans, are. However, His determination to surrender to God's perfect will was the choice He made. It is a lesson to us. God does not deny that we may be afraid or anxious; He never said our choices would be easy; but, like Jesus, we can trust that He knows best, even when it will cause us pain.

In the midst of all the pressure on His mind and spirit, Jesus (being aware of the trials the disciples would shortly be facing), strongly urged them to fight the flesh and pray, to keep themselves from falling into temptation. We often look down on the disciples because they couldn't stay awake, but remember it had been a long day and a long night. They would have been very tired.

HIS ARREST
READ MATTHEW 26: 47 – 56, LUKE 22: 47 – 53, and JOHN 18: 1 – 11
Combining these three accounts, summarize the events surrounding Jesus' arrest. _____

_____

_____

_____

_____

I have often wondered why Jesus' confirmation that He was indeed Jesus of Nazareth should cause the arresting party to draw back and fall to the ground. One exegetical commentary [19] pointed out that in the original Greek when Jesus first confirmed who He was, He had responded with the emphatic Name of God "I AM". It would suggest that the power resident in that Name spoken by the One who owned it resulted in the crowd falling back. The second time He said, "I am he" – thus drawing attention away from His followers and bringing it solely unto Him. His concern for their safety was evidently still uppermost in His mind.

Jesus asked a very valid question in Luke 22: 52. It speaks volumes that the leaders chose the cover of darkness when the crowds that usually followed Him were not around. True to their plot, they came to get Him while He was alone. Their first stop was before Annas, the father- in- law of the high priest.

HIS TRIAL
READ JOHN 18: 12 – 14

A number of bible commentaries point out that Annas had previously been high priest but was deposed by the Romans. Some believe that because of this the Jews might have still viewed Him as the true high priest. Others suggest that he may simply have had the respect of the office, having once held the position (akin to say a Professor Emeritus), and so his views and recommendations were sought first.

At any rate, notice that Jesus was bound (despite no evidence of Him resisting arrest) and brought to him.

READ JOHN 18: 15 – 27, & compare to MARK 14: 53 – 65

The other disciple mentioned in John 18: 15 is not named but is believed to be John and, if so, would explain his gospel giving added information about Jesus' trial, over that given in the synoptics. NIV points out that John 18: 24 may be translated in one of two ways: -

1. "Then Annas sent Him, still bound, to Caiaphas the high priest." Or
2. "(Now Annas had sent Him, still bound, to Caiaphas the high priest.)"

If translated as in a., it means that Annas was being referred to as high priest up to that point (e.g. verse 19 and 23) and the meeting of the Sanhedrin recorded in the synoptic gospels occurred after Annas sent Jesus on to Caiaphas. It would also mean the questioning he, Annas, carried out was illegal because no witnesses bringing accusations were mentioned.

I am more inclined to agree with the alternative translation because Caiaphas and not Annas was in fact high priest, and the correlation of his questioning Jesus while Peter denied Him matches the record in the synoptic gospels. Either way, we see the abuse of the Lord had already begun with the slap across His face. Another good reason for going with

---

the first translation is the fact that in John's gospel, Jesus had made a response to the high priest but the other gospels said He did not open His mouth. At the same time, it may have been that He just never responded to the specific accusations that were being brought against Him [Mark 14: 60].

- Why do you think Peter denied knowing Jesus? _____
  _____

Recall in chapter 9 of our study, we pointed out that the Sanhedrin was the Jewish ruling council. This then was Jesus' trial before the judiciary. Given the fact that this was being held in the high priest's home in secret in the dead of night, one must question its legality. Worse, by Jewish law, one could only be convicted on the testimony of at least two witnesses; and none of the witnesses' statements were in agreement. As a result their judgment finally hung on Jesus' declaration that He was the Christ [Mark 14: 62], which was the truth. However, they had already decided he wasn't and so ruled it as blasphemy. The sentence handed down was death [Matt. 26: 66]… and the abuse intensified. Jesus was blindfolded, repeatedly thumped and spat on, while being taunted and mocked.

There was one hitch in their plans, however. Under Rome, the Jews could not carry out the death penalty.

JUDAS' FATE
READ MATTHEW 27: 1 – 10
When was the death sentence passed [vs. 1]? _____

BEFORE ROME
READ JOHN 18: 28 – 38, then LUKE 23: 1 – 16
Write down your observations.

_____
_____
_____
_____
_____
_____

To summarize, since His arrest during the night, Jesus had been taken before Annas, the former high priest (a preliminary enquiry?); then on to Caiaphas and the entire Sanhedrin. He had been slapped across the face and spat upon while blindfolded – clearly an abuse of state powers. He was then taken to Pontius Pilate, the Roman governor, who tried to pass Him off to Herod. This latter only wanted to have Him "perform" for him and, when that wasn't forthcoming, returned Him to Pilate. Neither could find Him guilty of any crime deserving death … and all this on Friday morning, long before the sun had reached its zenith. His crime? Saying He was the Messiah.

Luke 23: 16 is shocking in that, despite the fact that Pilate found Him "Not Guilty", for political expediency in an effort to keep the peace, he was prepared to have Him flogged. For what??!

Given the beatings so far, what do you think Jesus' face looked like at this point? _____
_____

Remember also that He would have had nothing to eat or drink since the Passover meal the evening before.

We will break here for today, but let us not forget that on that fateful day, Jesus had no reprieve. Though tired, hungry, thirsty, weak and in pain, the agony was just beginning. The Passion week has been the subject of many sermons and films. As we have looked thus far on the events as they unfolded, is there anything that you have discovered for the first time? What are your thoughts right now?

PRAYER: -

Lord, I cannot begin to voice my gratitude for the sacrifice You made for me ... for me! God, I get so angry when I see the innocent suffering and not getting justice. Yet, You were innocent but still You chose, (as difficult and painful as it was for You), You **chose** to take my place. No words can even come close to declaring what that means... but thank You! Let me not forget, Lord.

CHAPTER 33

FOR THIS HE CAME

Let us continue our look at that dark day.

THE FINAL VERDICT

READ MATTHEW 27: 15 – 26
Write your thoughts. _____
_____
_____
_____

READ JOHN 19: 2 – 16
- Put yourself among the crowd as an onlooker. Describe the scene (think of the sounds, the look on Pilate's face, Jesus' appearance, etc.). _____
_____
_____
_____
_____
_____

- What would you have done if you had been in Pilate's position?
_____
_____
_____

THE SCOURGING

Matthew, Mark and John record in a single statement that Jesus was flogged. This doesn't begin to really describe what the Lord would have had to endure. In fact, from what we have read so far, He had already been struck repeatedly even before this flogging. So already, Jesus' face would have been bruised and swollen in areas, especially around the eyes where the skin is thin and delicate, and richly supplied with blood.

It is likely that haematomas (swellings formed from bleeding from the capillaries into the tissues under the skin, giving rise to a "black and blue" appearance) would have caused His eyes to be almost swollen shut. The eyes themselves would likely appear "blood-shot". His lips would have been dried, cracked and bleeding. There may even have been small lacerations (cuts) with bleeding in His mouth, caused by the teeth making sharp contact with the gums and cheeks from the punches to His face.

Now add to that the flogging. The Romans seemed to have mastered the art of scourging. Jesus would have been stripped and His hands tied to a post in front of Him, His back bared to His torturer. The Roman legionnaire would have then used a flagellum – a short whip consisting of a number of heavy leather thongs, the ends of which were knotted around small pieces of bone or jagged pieces of metal – to whip the Lord across His shoulders, back and legs.

This would have been done repeatedly so though initially, even putting aside the intense pain, there may have been welts and scratches; increasingly it would tear away pieces of skin, digging deeper and deeper. Eventually, His back would be a tangled bloody mess. Imagine throwing a robe unto a back in that condition… and add the crown of thorns to the tender flesh of His scalp. Let's not delve into what effect the actual crucifixion would have had on Him. Suffice it to say He would have been in unbearable pain and agony, and having great difficulty breathing. The purpose of this description was to get you thinking more deeply about what actually occurred. The prophet Isaiah saw it centuries before.

READ ISAIAH 52: 13 – 53: 12

Pause here for a moment and think about this very graphic picture. 52: 14 tells us that [at His crucifixion] His appearance appalled those who looked at Him, so disfigured and "marred" beyond human recognition was He (because of the way they tortured Him),as we will soon see. 53: 4 points out that people assumed that God was punishing Him, and it is true that it was God who purposed and willed His death. The totality of God's wrath against sin was poured upon Jesus as He was made (became) sin [2 Corinth. 5: 21]… but God was not punishing *Him*. In actuality He was "pierced" and "crushed" for *our* sins! "By His wounds we are healed." Look through this passage again slowly and picture in your mind what Isaiah saw.

HIS CRUCIFIXION

READ LUKE 23: 26 – 43 & JOHN 19: 17 – 27

Record your observations.

_____

_____

_____

_____

_____

Now, let us look at it from Jesus' perspective.

READ PSALM 22: 1 – 21

Can you picture how the mob calling for His death would appear as bulls and lions and dogs? Can you feel the drop in His stomach; the "butterflies" from the anxiety of His impending flogging and crucifixion; His bones feeling out of joint, hanging on the cross? Being so dehydrated and having lost so much blood, can you understand His tongue sticking to the roof of His mouth?

People, realize that God was saying, "This is the just penalty for sin; this is the only appropriate punishment for what sin deserves." And a gracious

God knew we could never pay that price… so He sent One who could. Nevertheless, note the triumph at the end. Psalm 22: 31 is indeed true:

"They will proclaim His righteousness to a people yet unborn – for He has done it."

HALLELUJAH!!!

HIS DEATH

READ MATTHEW 27: 45 – 56 & compare to JOHN 19: 28 – 37
- What events occurred at the moment of Jesus' death? _____

_____

- Is there anything else in these narratives that stand out to you?

_____

_____

- List the women named who were standing at the foot of the cross.

_____

Recall **Isaiah 53: 4 – 6:**

> *"Surely He took up our infirmities and carried our sorrows, yet we considered Him stricken by God, smitten by Him and afflicted. But He was pierced for our transgressions, He was crushed for our iniquities; the punishment that brought us peace was upon Him, and by His wounds we are healed. We all, like sheep, have gone astray, each of us has turned to his own way; and the Lord has laid on Him the iniquity of us all." (Memory verse)*

HIS BURIAL

READ JOHN 19: 38 – 42 & compare to LUKE 23: 50 – 56
- Note the two individuals who took Jesus' body for burial. What did they have in common [see Luke 23: 50 & John 3: 1]? _____

_____

- Recapping all the events of that Friday, write a summary here. ____

_____

_____

_____

_____

_____

_____

_____

> **BRAATA: -**
> All the gospels make note of the fact that the women who had closely followed Jesus were very much present at His crucifixion. All, except Luke, name them. It is unclear if John was indicating four women or three (Jesus' aunt then being Mary, the wife of Clopas). I doubt the latter, because I think it unlikely that one family would have two daughters named Mary in it. Looking at it in conjunction with Matthew's and Mark's records, Salome may have been the name of His aunt and she may therefore have been the mother of Zebedee's sons. This would make James and John (the sons of Zebedee) cousins of Jesus. Alternatively, she may have been another woman entirely, just not identified in the other gospels.
> Nevertheless, these women were there at the end and, as we will see, were there at the new beginning.

Saturday

READ MATTHEW 27: 62 – 66
The elders left nothing to chance. Yet, this in itself would help to prove that no-one had stolen the body of the Lord.

Well, friends – I know we have covered a lot today, and given the nature of what we have looked at, most of us may be feeling quite drained right now. It must have been a long, distressing, depressing, and emotional day for the Lord and all His followers. Evil reigned and believed it was victorious.

How could this be?
It makes no sense;
My mind just cannot comprehend
The angel said You came as King
To free us...end our suffering

Our hopes were raised, our spirits soared
We had such high expectations, Lord.
Now, all is dark, we see no light;
All is pain, no end in sight.

We walk in fear... downcast, tense
How could this be?
It makes no sense!

Mary's Question –
By Michelle Thompson 11/11/11

Child of God, how are you feeling right now? Pour out your heart to Him.

CHAPTER 34
"MY LORD & MY GOD"
➤ ❀ ❮

Sunday

READ MATTHEW 28: 1 – 15, LUKE 24: 1 – 12 & JOHN 20: 1 – 18
- Who were the first to see Jesus resurrected? _____

By the time the women had reached Jesus' tomb, at dawn on Sunday morning, He had risen!! Skeptics who refute the resurrection like to point out that Friday afternoon to early Sunday morning does not equal three days. However, we need to be cognizant of the fact that the Jewish day begins at 6:00 p.m. (hence, in Genesis, it states that the evening and the morning were the first day). Therefore, 6:01 p.m. on Friday was the beginning of the second day, and so on. This is why it was necessary to take Jesus down from the cross because it was the Preparation for the Sabbath, which commenced at 6:00 p.m.!

It strikes me that, despite all Jesus had foretold, it is obvious that none of them expected Him to actually rise again that Sunday. Even when they discovered the body missing, resurrection was the last thing on their minds. Mary Magdalene's devotion is evident; and she was rewarded – she was the first one to see the risen Lord. She is named in all the accounts but it is clear that she was accompanied by other women as they went to anoint His body with spices.

READ LUKE 24: 13 – 35

So, John's gospel tells us Mary Magdalene was the first to see the risen Lord. Later that same day (Sunday), He appears to two other disciples, one of whom is identified as Cleopas. We are not told who the other was.

- What do we discover about the faith of these two disciples in verses 19 – 24? _____
- What did the "stranger" teach them as they travelled to Emmaus?

  _____
- When did they recognize Jesus? _____
- From vs. 34, who do we learn was the second one to see the risen Christ? _____

Passages like these confirm for me the truth of the testimonies, because they made no effort to make anybody look good; they just told it like it was. The disappointment, disbelief and discouragement of the disciples are all laid bare for everyone to see. Their recounting of the events concerning Jesus all spoke of hope in the past tense. They said that Jesus **was** a prophet; they **had hoped** He would redeem Israel; and even though the women reported that the angel had said He was alive, their disbelief was evident even as they pointed out that they had not seen Him.

This passage also explains for us the reason the disciples (later apostles) could clearly speak to the prophecies of the Old Testament (O.T.) that find their fulfillment in Jesus. Jesus gave them a fantastic bible study [vs. 27] on their way to Emmaus. He illuminated all the scriptures from the O.T. that concerned Him.

It strikes me that their eyes were opened to recognize Him when He carried out an act that would have been familiar to them: He gave thanks and broke bread with them. I believe His mannerisms revealed Him. What do you think? We also learn from their testimony to the "Eleven" (the term now used to refer to the core group of disciples who had followed Him closely) that Simon Peter had already seen the Lord too (confirmed in 1 Corinthians 15:5). Notice too that although the term "Eleven" was used, it referred to the group in general and did not mean that all of them were present at the time, as we will soon see. (By the way, sometimes they were still called the Twelve, even though Judas was no longer with them. It's just easier than listing all of them by name).

READ LUKE 24: 36 – 49 & JOHN 20: 19 – 23

- Despite the testimony of the disciples above, what was the state of their faith? _____

- What observations can we make about the resurrection body from this passage? _____
_____
_____

- What did He do to enable them to believe? _____
_____
_____
_____

Given that in those days they usually discounted the testimonies of women; it could be considered understandable that they were still convinced that Jesus remained dead. Yet, they just could not believe it, even after these two disciples confirmed that He was alive (notwithstanding the fact that Jesus had told them before He died that all this would happen). Just as human as we are, they needed to see it for themselves!

John lets us know that it was Sunday evening that Jesus appeared to them; and that He came into the room unhindered by locked doors. Given the uncertainty of who He was at each appearance, it says to me that we will not look exactly the same when we are clothed in this new resurrected, incorruptible body. We will not be restricted by walls or locked doors, as He just appeared among them; and we will not be ghosts, but have flesh and bones. He was even able to eat with them.

The bible study is repeated for their benefit; and He opened their understanding so they could receive the revelation from the scriptures. This, by the way, He still does for us. Haven't you ever read a word of Scripture repeatedly and then as you dig deeper and seek Him, your mind is open to a deeper meaning; and you wonder how it is you never saw that before? I trust a lot of that has happened as you have gone through this study.

Do not miss the fact that He told them that all along the O.T. had indicated that, aside from the way He would suffer, repentance and forgiveness would be preached in His Name to *all* nations, beginning at Jerusalem (and that is exactly what we see played out in the book of Acts). From the beginning, the plan had always been to offer redemption to all mankind. In John's gospel, already we see them being commissioned to **GO**.

READ JOHN 20: 24 – 31
- Put yourself in Thomas' shoes. What would have been your reaction when you heard the testimonies of your friends? _____

  _____

- When did Thomas finally see the Lord? _____

Do you realize we are "those who have not seen and yet have believed"? John also lets us know that the reason all these things are recorded is for our sakes; that we too may believe what they were convinced of (*an dem did de de* i.e. and they were there!). Jesus is the Christ, the Son of God! With that belief, we too have life in His Name. Hallelujah!

READ JOHN 21: 1 – 14
- Who were the disciples present on this occasion? _____

  _____

- Does this story sound familiar? _____
- Where did we meet a similar occurrence? _____

  _____

- Do you think there is a lesson for the disciples in this account? If so, what? _____

  _____

  _____

My very active imagination pictures the disciples feeling like "a chicken without a head". Their leader had gone, and they were in "waiting mode", and I think some were getting tired of it. They just didn't want to sit around doing nothing. To me, Peter was effectively saying, *"Ier wa, mi gweehn go do wa mi nuo fi do... mi a go kech fish."* i.e. "Listen, I am going to do what I am familiar with... I'm going to go back to fishing." So this is what they went to do; but I believe this is not what the Lord had called them to do, so they caught nothing... until the Lord gave them the direction as to where to fish.

Now let's be realistic, it truly shouldn't matter whether you cast your net on one side of the boat or the other... it is the same water underneath, after all! But remember the last time this happened? Look back at the calling of the first disciples in chapter 7 of our study. In Luke 5: 1 – 11, before Peter, James and John had become His followers, they had toiled all night fishing and had caught nothing. Then Jesus told them to put out into the deep, and the result was that their nets almost broke from the weight of all the fish they caught. Others had to come and help them. It was at that time that Jesus had told Peter that "from now on you will catch men".

I believe that in this incident in John's gospel, Jesus needed to remind them what they were called to – to be fishers of men, not fishermen. John would have remembered the first calling, and so He recognized the Lord. Isn't it typical of Him to remind without condemning? John records that this was the third appearance of Jesus to His disciples.

READ JOHN 21: 15 – 25
- What thoughts run through your mind as you read this passage?

_____
_____
_____
_____

It is not clear from the passage what the word "these" represents in Christ's question to Peter. Some believe it is the boats, nets and other fishing paraphernalia; some think the Lord is asking if Peter loves Him more than he does his friends, the other disciples; and still others think Jesus is asking Peter if he loves the Lord more than the other disciples do. We don't really know for sure which; but I believe it may be the last option given that Peter had earlier insisted that "even if all fall away" on account of Jesus, *he* never would [Matt. 26: 33]. He then subsequently denied Jesus, in the midst of His greatest need.

It is noted also that in the original Greek, two different words are used for the word "love", hence the NIV translating it "truly love" and "love". Jesus therefore asks Peter the first two times if he (Peter) has an all-encompassing, sacrificial love (agape) for Him, and Peter responds all three times that he is absolutely fond of Him (phileo). As we would say in Jamaica, Peter was essentially saying, *"Yu an mi a brejrin, Laad."* (i.e. "We are like brothers"). On the third occasion of asking, Jesus used the word "phileo", not pressing the point. Peter would come to understand later on in his ministry. Some believe this is just typical of the way John writes and that we should attach no deeper meaning to the different word used. What are your thoughts?

Jesus therefore asks Peter three times if he really loves Him, to which he responds in the affirmative, becoming hurt that the Lord repeats the question. Notice that Peter's responses no longer held the pride and self-righteousness that was there before. He simply affirmed the truth of his love for the Lord. Maybe He wanted Peter to realize that He knows that he, Peter, does love Him; and that He had no "hard feelings" towards him for denying Him. With each response of Peter, the Lord reaffirms His call on his life to shepherd His flock… to fish for and feed men (and women). In fact, He prophecies that it will cost him his life [vs. 19]. Simon Peter would be left in no doubt that he remained a part of Jesus. I believe Peter had grown and this transformation was necessary for the awesome task ahead of him – shepherding the Lord's sheep.

I love how Peter, being so typical of us humans, wants to know "what about him (John)?" We don't want to think that we alone will have to sacrifice or suffer. Jesus tells him "mind your own business" – a timely word to us too. Focus on your call and task, and stop watching other people.

John finally confirms that it is he who is testifying to all these things and has written them down. He assures us it is the truth, the whole truth and nothing but the truth.

PRAYER: -

1. Pray for your church – that divisions will cease and we will fulfill the Lord's prayer of being one as He and the Father are one.
2. For your bible study group/ prayer group – that the Word of God will transform you, making you more & more like Him; and filling you with power to change the world for Him.
3. For you - that your love for Him may grow deeper as you come to know Him, and that nothing will pluck you from His hand.
4. For anything else on your heart.

CHAPTER 35
UNTIL HE COMES, GO!

READ MATTHEW 28: 16 – 20

- What do we learn from Jesus' opening words here? _____
  _____

- What does the commission to the disciples involve? _____
  _____
  _____
  _____
  _____

After Jesus' resurrection we saw where He had sent a message to the disciples telling them to go into Galilee where they would see Him [Matt. 28: 10]. In this passage we see them with Him at the designated meeting place, and here He gives them what has come to be known as the Great Commission. Notice that Jesus declares that **all** authority both in heaven and on earth has been given to Him i.e. He rules over **all**.

READ PHILIPPIANS 2: 5 – 11

- What had been Jesus' attitude? _____
  _____
  _____

- What was the result of His complete obedience? _____
  _____
  _____

Jesus, though being God, did not resent giving up that position; and not only did He become mortal/human but He even submitted Himself to the humiliation and agony of being killed by crucifixion. As a result of His complete obedience at all cost, God exalted Him to the highest position and place of authority so that everything and everyone in heaven and on earth and under the earth – **all** – now fall under His authority, and will bow to Him.

> **BRAATA:**
> For the extent of His dominion, see Revelation 1: 17 – 18 & 11: 15.
> What Satan sought to get through rebellion [see Ezekiel 28: 12 – 17; Luke 10: 18; & Rev. 12: 7 – 12]. Jesus gained through obedience and submission to God the Father.

Returning to Matt. 28: 19 & 20: Jesus now has the authority over everything. Satan has no legal ground unless we give it up to him. Therefore, Jesus sent the disciples to testify and gain followers from every nation – all peoples – and confirm their union with God's family by their baptism. The disciples were charged with teaching these people so they could follow in obedience and in turn, increase the kingdom.

Finally, He promised His presence with them (and us) until He returns at the end of the age.

So, flashback with me:

After centuries of looking for the Messiah, the promised Redeemer, Israel had settled into complacency and the commonplace. This was interrupted by visitors – messengers from heaven, declaring the coming of not just the Messiah, but His forerunner, the one who would prepare the way. And so we saw the Lord coming to earth, taking on human flesh with all its frailties, in the form of a tiny baby.

Despite such humble beginnings, He had lowly shepherds and Eastern Magi ("kings") seeking Him. The "silent" years of His childhood are interrupted only by a glimpse of Him at age 12 in the temple, already cognizant of His Father's call upon Him, yet submitting to His earthly parents. Then we later saw Him launching out into His ministry, the way having been prepared by John the Baptist.

He calls His disciples and then begins to turn Jerusalem and its environs "right side up" with His teachings and miraculous signs. He challenges the leaders and the people to correctly understand God's heart and obey Him. The "love affair/honeymoon" soon fades as His teachings and his stance begin to make Him enemies; but He would not compromise the truth. His heart for the downtrodden and those seeking justice was evident, as He reflected His Father's heart. He had no patience for the proud and self-righteous; those who were more concerned about appearances than the actual state of their heart. As a result, His enemies increased as did their desire to be rid of him, even as His following increased.

As the time for His death approached, we saw Him begin to prepare His disciples for what was to come and also for what God's Kingdom and the final judgment entailed. What the enemy intended as defeat became the greatest victory ever won. Jesus triumphed over sin, death and the grave – defeating Satan and freeing the human race from his hold over us. Jesus rose victorious, having taken captivity captive. We have been made free, at last! God's original plan for relationship with mankind has been restored, a way having been made to bring together a holy God and a people trapped in sin. *God intervened in history to draw mankind unto Himself.*

Luke, the author of the book of Luke and the book of Acts, and the consummate historian, gives us a bit more information about the events at the time of Christ's ascension into heaven.

READ ACTS 1: 1 – 11
What information do you glean from this passage? _____
_____
_____
_____

Here, we are told that the Lord showed Himself repeatedly to quite a number of His disciples over a period of forty days, giving them proof that He was indeed alive. From verse 6 we still see remnants of them expecting an earthly kingdom – the restoration of Israel as a sovereign nation. Jesus told them to "get over it" (my words); to let the Father do what He wants to do; but wait for the baptism of the Holy Spirit and with Him, power that will enable them to become witnesses starting in their immediate environs (Jerusalem and Judea, then Samaria), and extending to the whole world.

Then before their very eyes, he ascended into heaven. Notice the angel told them to get moving; He will return in the same way they saw Him go up... as we saw before, His second coming will be evident for all to see.

Well, friends, that is it. How have you found the journey? Do you know this Jesus better now than when you started? Has this study brought you closer to Him than you were before? Do you have a deeper respect and reverence for Him? It is my prayer that you can now say with certainty that you do really love Him. If you were not a Christian when you started, I trust you have made that step. If you have not but would like to make that step now, pray this prayer with me now:

> *Father, Your word says that all have sinned and fall short of Your glory. I know that all my efforts to gain righteousness have been futile; it is only by the sacrifice of Jesus that I am truly washed clean, forgiven of every sin and brought back into relationship with You. I am so grateful for the sacrifice He made for me. I confess to you that what You say is true – I am a sinner. Please forgive me and cleanse me and accept me into the body of Christ. By Your Spirit, help me to understand Your Word and cause that it transforms me and restores me in the image of Jesus. I surrender to You completely, Lord. I love You.*
>
> *Amen.*

If you just said that prayer, welcome to the Kingdom of the Sovereign God. I urge you to find a fellowship (i.e. church) near you that rightly teaches the Word of God, where you can be properly discipled, much like the Lord Jesus taught and prepared His disciples. Keep close to the Lord, study His Word, and hold fast to Him, despite the tests that you may face. His Word is true: He is coming again, and soon.

READ REVELATION 22: 12 – 21

Amen. Come Lord Jesus!

GROUP STUDY GUIDE

Group Study- week 1

A. *On day 1 of our study, we read that Jesus was called the Word, through which the world was created. Read and discuss the following passages:*
   James 3: 3 - 12
   Psalm 64: 3
   Proverbs 18: 21
   What conclusions can be drawn?
B. *Discuss the lessons learnt from Jesus' ancestry. Did these cause you to look at your own in a different light? If so, how?*
C. *In chapter 3, we saw that John the Baptist did not view himself as "Elijah" but Jesus did. What about you? Does your vision of yourself line up with God's perception of you?*
D. *Talk about what you learnt from the study this week. Discuss challenges as well as insights.*

Group Study - week 2

This week we looked at the people Jesus called to follow Him and noticed He "doesn't call the qualified, but rather qualifies the called". Do you know what spiritual gift/gifts God has given to you? Do you recognize His call upon your life?

What have been some of the obstacles you have or are facing?

Has the study this week encouraged you to move past these? What else have you learnt?

Group Study - week 3

Discussion points:

A. *How is your life making an impact on those around you? How is your witness? Do others know you are a Christian?*
B. *Discuss practical ways to spread the Good News in your present circumstances and surroundings.*
C. *Based on our study on the Lord's prayer, is there anyone you need to forgive?*
D. *Discuss Jesus' "mission statement" in Luke 4: 18 - 19. What thoughts does it inspire regarding your mission?*
E. *How would you describe Jesus based on our study so far?*

Group Study - week 4

A. *Have you ever been in the position of having to tell someone the truth, even though you know that truth may hurt them or cause them to hate you? What was the outcome? What lessons did you learn from the experience(s)?*
B. *Has someone ever had to tell you a painful truth?*
C. *Have you been feeling God calling you to completely surrender to Him - your choices, your will, your plans, your future...your life? What is your response?*
D. *How does your family compare or contrast with Jesus' earthly family? Share your experiences.*
E. *Having seen what His family was like, how do you now feel about yours?*

Group Study - week 5

Discuss some of the lessons learned this past week: coming to conclusions based on assumptions, possible areas of bondage in your life, and letting go of some long-held "treasures" that may be hindering the work and move of God in your life.

Is there something you have been waiting on for a long time? Have you given up hope, or given up on God? Did you hear God speaking to you this week about it? Did you seek Him for His will concerning it?

Look again at Ezekiel 34: 1 - 10. What important truths about leadership can we learn?

Group study - week 6

What does it mean to you, practically, to surrender/lay down your life for Him?

What are the features of a leader, taking Jesus as your example?

Consider the first 2 chapters of Job and Jesus' warning and assurance to Peter that Satan had requested permission to test the disciples. Discuss.

Look at Hebrews 10: 26 - 39 and Romans 11: 17 - 22. What conclusions can be drawn from these passages?

Group study - week 7

Discuss the lessons learnt this past week.

Recap important points or challenges from the study. Plan to continue meeting regularly for bible study!

BIBLIOGRAPHY

Introduction

1   NIV Study Bible. The time between the Testaments.
2   The Silent Centuries. The Maccabean Revolt (168- 135 BC) by Al Maxey.

Chapter 1

3   The Names of God. Study by J. Hampton Keathley, III; Bible.org
4   NIV Study Bible- notes on Gen. 1: 1.

Chapter 2

5   "Gematria is the practice of giving each letter in the alphabet a numeric value, and then seeking to determine the symbolic meaning of the numbers of some name or event or place. The name David in Hebrew adds up to the number fourteen." -The genealogy of Jesus by Al Maxey; Oct. 16, 2012; www.gracecentral.com/genealogy-of-Jesus.htm
6   Wikipedia- The Genealogy of Jesus.
7   Helpmewithbiblestudy.org: What's in a name? A look at Genealogies.
8   Life of Christ: Genealogy of Jesus Christ. www.lifeofchrist.com/life/genealogy/print.html: Luke's Genealogy of Jesus. Joseph in Christ's Genealogy.

Chapter 9

9   Sanhedrin- Wikipedia, the free encyclopedia; en.wikipedia.org/wiki/Sanhedrin

10   The Sanhedrin by Shira Schoenberg. Jewish Virtual Library; A Division of The American-Israeli Cooperative Enterprise

11   NIV Study Bible; notes on Mark 14: 55.

Chapter 10

12   New Testament Survey: Bible study and Commentary prepared by Joe T. White; Volume 2 – Luke/John; pg. 63.

Chapter 13

13   There was also the consideration of the people hearing Him being affirmed by Satan's servants... the demons. The Pharisees also tried to use this to discredit Him [Matt. 12: 24].

Chapter 26

14   NIV Study bible notes on Daniel 11: 21.

Chapter 28

15   The Passover – Celebrating Our Salvation. www.churchisraelforum.com/the_passover_celebrating_our_salvation.htm

16   The Four Cups of Wine of Passover<<Possessing the Treasure 26 Mar. 2008. Mikeratliff.wordpress.com/2008/03/26/the-four-cups-of-wine-of-passover/.

17   The Four Cups of Wine for Passover/Pesach. www.angelfire.com/pa2/passover/thefourcupsofwineforpassover.html

Chapter 29

18   Vine's Complete Expository Dictionary of Old and New Testament Words. W. E. Vine, Merril F. Unger, William White, JR. Glorify.

Chapter 32

19   Exegetical Commentary on John 18. Bible.org/seriespage/exegetical-commentary-john-18.

Printed in the United States
By Bookmasters